The
Text Book

Tips, Quips, and Scripts
to help you text better.

Written By: Elizabeth Rossi

ISBN: 9781987627893 Paperback

Library of Congress Control Number (LCCN):

Printed and bound in the United States of America. First printing, June 2019. First Edition. Second printing, September 2019. Second Edition.

Publisher: KD Publishing, United States.

Distributed by: Amazon.com and book resellers worldwide.

For information about special discounts available for bulk purchases, sales promotions, and educational needs, visit: **www.the-text-book.com** and complete the contact form.

TABLE OF CONTENTS

FOREWORD

When I was a little girl around four years old, I remember sitting on the green shag rug in the family room of my parent's house, in the small town of Wexford, Pennsylvania. It was a typical Saturday morning, and I was glued to whatever cartoons were currently blaring from the television set.

My older brother Pete sat down next to me at the edge of the wooden coffee table and said to get ready for kindergarten that I should know how to write my name. He had brought over crayons and scratch paper, and patiently showed me how to write out the lines for each letter to spell, B E T H.

Granted it was using "Cornflower Blue"... but that was my first-ever memory of writing anything. So this book is dedicated to my brother Peter J. Rossi. May you be looking down from heaven with pride. We love and miss you every day.

To all of my family, mom and dad, Rich and Sherrie, Tony and Stephanie, Joe and his cat, Karis, and Josh... I'm so grateful for each of you, knowing you, and being a part of the Rossi family clan.

To the countless people that I have crossed paths with, who have in some way shaped me into the person I've become and helped develop and refine my communication skills, from friends, boyfriends, family, colleagues, teachers, other authors, and even strangers.

Thank you all for your continued love, never-ending support, advice and guidance through my creative development process with each new film and tv script, song, and now book! My sincerest hope is to reflect back to you the love and light that you have given me.

Our communication ways and styles will continue to evolve, and I hope this book helps them evolve for the better... to express ourselves fully and completely, in loving and kind ways, that help to build bridges and authentic connections.

1

INTRODUCTION

Hi and thanks for purchasing *The Text Book*! I sincerely hope that the lessons and suggestions contained within these pages help you with whatever texting situation you're currently in.

Just the fact that you've researched, found, and bought this book shows that you are seeking help – which isn't recognizing the need for help half the battle? The mere fact this book is in your hands is a key that you are looking to improve your communication skills and learn new ways to express your feelings and ideas in the best manner possible.

This book will help you not only text better; it will help you be a better communicator overall. We'll look at common pitfalls of texting and electronic communication, overall texting manners and etiquette, and go through some texting lessons and ways that will help you discover and convey the point that you're really trying to make.

These lessons and communication methods are effective no matter your age, gender, race, whether you've sent a million text messages or if you are sending your first one.

By the end of this book, you'll have a better understanding of the intended meaning behind the texts that you send and be able to communicate that meaning better. Better communication will improve all areas of life... work relationships, love relationships, and friendships will benefit from reading these lessons and putting them to good use.

Why I Wrote The Text Book

Being a writer, I've grown accustomed over the years to friends, family, and colleagues continuously approaching me seeking writing advice with business letters, resumes, and with private and sometimes difficult and stressful situations.

They'd ask things like: What do I text if they say...? How can I phrase this better? Is there a way to address this text message/situation without them getting defensive?

During those conversations, I had learned how to derive what their actual intention was behind the situation and what it was that they were genuinely looking to express. Then I'd help them convey the true intended meaning into drafted messages to use, and the messages worked! They achieved their desired outcomes by revealing their authentic intentions in a way that was positive and loving, even when the scenario itself was wearisome, offensive, or uncertain.

I began to recognize there is a real need out there. People are seeking ways to express what they are feeling and their ideas, in hopes of building authentic connections and improve relationships, but they're just not sure what to say sometimes or the best way to say it to achieve the desired outcomes.

Unfortunately, we're not taught these types of communication skills. Many people learn through experience or circumstances, to repress their deepest thoughts and feelings, trying to always please others first, or they are simply afraid to acknowledge and say what's really on their hearts and minds.

Poor communication between friends, family, co-workers, and lovers, can lead to resentment, bitterness, frustration, anger, and worse... the loss of connection and breakdown within that relationship.

Even still in these situations, there is still hope.

With the right words, one text message has the potential to make an impact that can change the course of an entire life.

The impact from a single text message can produce positive or negative results depending on the chosen words, which makes it even more crucial to learn to communicate effectively whether via text, email, or in-person.

So after many years of experience of helping people draft letters, emails, and text messages, I've decided to share the communication tips I've learned and shared with my own friends, family, and colleagues, and have tailored this information for use with one of the most common communication platforms available today... texting.

Hopefully, people across the globe can and will improve their texting and communication skills overall from this book, as we continue to evolve into a population that is ever more reliant on electronic communications.

Getting the Most From this Guide

Considering you've made it this far in the Introduction and Overview, I feel confident you will read this book cover to cover, which ultimately is the best way to garner all of the advice and suggestions held within these pages.

Even if you are an experienced texter and familiar with all of the technological functions and tasks, I'd still recommend skimming the first chapter, "Texting Basics 101". You may discover a tip that will be useful, and because you consider yourself a text-master, there's a greater chance you have a not-so-savvy older relative who needs help. So you'll also be able to use the Texting Basics 101 chapter as a reference tool with easy ways to explain those how-tos for the texting newbies.

After reading this book through cover to cover once, you may want to keep it handy as a reference guide. The lessons will be helpful reminders on how to discover the intended meaning behind your text messages and cross-reference with the quips, scripts, and texting templates that you can use time and time again to craft meaningful messages.

Are you unsure whether or not to send a text? Refer to the Text-iquette section for suggestions on texting manners, etiquette, and what may or may not be appropriate.

Needing help on what to write in your text message? Refer to the latter half of the book for texting templates and sample text messages that are ready-to-send. These are broken apart by mood/occasion and are perfect for when you have that texter's block! Use one of the scripts as-is or create a more personalized version by using a texting template.

"Death and life are in the

power of the tongue."

~ Ancient Proverb

2

TEXTING BASICS

Learning something new can be daunting and technology is ever-changing, so hats off to you for taking on the challenge and expanding your personal horizons.

Texting basics will help to demystify this 160-character instant message and hopefully explain a thing or two about this modern-day communication method, even to the savviest of texters. For texting newbies, we'll cover some of the day-to-day text necessities, as well as some of the most common questions circulating about texting, such as:

- How to know if your text message actually went through - was it delivered? Was it read?

- What is the difference between SMS and MMS? How do you switch between them? Why would you want to?

- What is the 'best' way to save attachments and photos, so they don't get lost in cyberspace or accidentally deleted?

- Can I delay sending a text message until later?

For the purposes of this chapter, the answers and instructions to these questions are provided for Apple products and Android products. Based on the exact phone model the individual steps or icons may vary slightly, however, these steps should provide a launching point for any modern-day smartphone or similar device.

How Texting Got Its Start

Humankind has an innate desire... the desire to communicate and thereby connect with each other. We are born with a need to express ourselves and to be heard, truly heard.

Even the earliest findings of man include cave drawings depicting their struggles, expressing and communicating their lives at that moment in time. And while the method of communication has changed over time, this need hasn't. Each one of us is a unique creation, unlike anyone else in the world, and we each have our individual levels of this innate desire... and those levels will vary from minute to minute, and day to day, as our lives ebb and flow along their natural course.

Over time there have been many advances in the communication field, helping us to fulfil this desire. From the cave drawing and hieroglyphics used in ancient civilizations to the very first text message recorded in 1992, to the emoticons and multimedia messages used in modern-day texting.

In essence though, they're all the same - a brief message to express our thoughts and feelings, in an attempt to communicate and connect with another person.

If we define the modern-day text as a 'message that uses electrical signals conveyed via a dedicated telecommunication circuit between two people,' then from a historical perspective texting actually began in the early 19th century via the electrical telegraph, which was invented by Samuel Morse. Shortly after its creation in the 1840s, electrical telegraph networks enabled people to transmit messages across continents and oceans almost instantly. Sound familiar?

Morse and his code of dots and dashes revolutionized the communication industry. Since then, communications and protocols advanced over radio waves away from using Morse Code and through various other iterations, until the first Short Message Service (SMS) was sent on December 3, 1992, in the United Kingdom. The message simply read, "Merry Christmas."

Texting initially was off to a slow start those first several years, until cellular phone service providers began incorporating this feature as part of their standard mobile phone package in the late 1990's. The feature caught on quickly. It was estimated that in just over the first decade, revenue from texting topped $585 billion annually.

As with most major inventions, the world experiences a shift as it learns and adjusts, reaping the advantages of this new invention that makes our daily lives more comfortable and better in some way.

Texting is no different in this arena. It is helping people globally to express their thoughts, feelings, and ideas, faster than ever before, and helping to fulfil that innate desire within each of us to communicate and connect with each other.

In fact, the use of texting has been one of the fastest growing trends of our modern age, and the numbers are still growing, with more than 15 million texts being sent every minute worldwide according to 2017 statistics. *

There are downsides however to all of this instant communication. Misinterpretations of intent and related texting pitfalls that we should be aware and mindful of, so that the communication tool itself can be the best that it can be.

*https://www.textrequest.com/blog/texting-statistics-answer-questions/

The Purpose of Texting

Each tool has a purpose where it is used best. For example, you wouldn't use a hammer to turn a screw, and you wouldn't want to use a screwdriver as a hammer or to saw through wood. Each tool functions best when it is used correctly, for the situations and circumstances that it was invented.

Texting is also a tool that can and should be used in certain circumstances but may not appropriate or best suited for other situations. However, because of the convenience of texting, the lines for this particular tool have been blurred as it's commonality and usage continues to climb, crossing the threshold of its intended purpose.

Texts are an excellent way for people to instantly connect, reconnect, and communicate with each other. It helps families and friends stay and feel like they're a part of each other's lives, whether the family members live in the same house or on different continents.

Texts enable people to send photos, video, and other sentiments within the blink of an eye (usually!). They are excellent for quick updates, checking in, running late, and all sorts of other mini-messages.

That is the intended purpose of this communication tool... mini-messages of 160 characters or less. Texts are absolutely great in these circumstances and are incredibly convenient.

Text messages are not great for extended conversations, long notes, anything involving complicated tasks, or expressing deep emotions, or complicated feelings.

In each of these cases... texts often create more havoc.

Using text messages in these situations is like trying to use a saw when you should be using a screwdriver. Texting for extended or complicated conversations will result in any number and assortment of pitfalls, and miscommunications which we will cover in later chapters.

Unless you are specifically looking to add chaos and drama to your life, I recommend to text quick and uncomplicated messages, and to use the other tools of communication we still have at our fingertips for deeper and longer conversations.

The good news is that much of the communication advice available in this book will help regardless of the communication method, so do not fear!

When to Text vs. Email vs. Phone

The standard text message has a 160-character limit. This limit was imposed for a reason… texts are meant to be mini-messages, not electronic novels. Below are some general guidelines to consider, if and when you are wondering if texting is the best tool to use for your message:

- If your text message requires more than 480 characters (3 standard SMS texts), consider perhaps an email. At the very least, be sure and switch to an MMS message, so that your thoughts aren't broken apart into several 160-character texts that will arrive in a random order, leaving the receiver to piece together the original message like a puzzle.

- If your text message regards a significant life decision, such as career, health, or marriage, consider a phone call.

- If you are having a hard time articulating how or what to say because the subject is difficult to explain, it may be misperceived in a text message. Consider an email or phone call based on the situation.

- If you have complicated feelings regarding a relationship and want to express them, consider a phone call. Love is too important to leave to the pitfalls and miscommunications that can happen over texting.

- If you have sent a message and the response exchanges go beyond 4x, and either party still has questions from the first initial topic, consider an email with a bulleted list of instructions or a phone call. It will alleviate the confusion and save time.

How to Send a Basic Text Message

There are many different applications, or "apps," available on the market today that are explicitly geared towards texting.

Smartphones typically come preinstalled with several texting application options. Usually, the carrier (Verizon, Sprint, AT&T, T-Mobile, etc.) will have their own branded texting app, and the manufacturer (Samsung, Google, Apple, etc.) will have also offer a texting app. Text messages sent using this type of app are sent to the receiver, using the carrier's global network and require either a monthly plan, which can have an allotted number of text messages per month or can be unlimited. Some service providers will also offer a pay per text option.

There are also plenty of texting options available online for sending and receiving instant messages with tools such as WhatsApp, Slacker, Skype, Snapchat, and more. These messaging options require an internet connection and can specifically be useful for international texting and calling, and in remote areas where the carriers' network service is low or non-existent.

While all of these texting apps vary slightly in design, layout, and color, there isn't much variation with the actual "how to" part of sending a message.

STEP BY STEP LESSON #1

Here are the basic steps of how to create and send a new text message to a receiver:

- Open the texting application of choice and enter a phone number or name in the "To:" field. This will be the person who receives the text message.

- Alternatively, select a contact from your phone's contact list and tap the chat message icon, which automatically will open the phone's default texting app with the "To:" field completed.

- Using the keypad on your phone, type a message in the "Message:" field.

- Tap the "Send" button, which can look like an arrow.

The message will now appear in the list of texting conversations, for easier sending and replying to that receiver.

Sending and Saving Attachments

Texting is a great way for quickly sending and sharing photos, videos, and more with your friends and family.

However, with all of the different applications that are being used to send and save those photos, how can you save them all to the same place and be sure that those precious memories are safely and securely stored?

STEP BY STEP LESSON #2

The instructions below focus on the basics of attaching a photo to a text message, saving a picture locally to the phone's internal storage, as well as the best way to securely store photos and other attachments in one place, so that they don't get lost or even accessed by unauthorized people.

Apple - How to send a photo:

- Open the iMessage application from the Home screen.

- Start a new message and tap the camera icon.

- Tap to take a photo.

- Tap Done and then tap Send.

Apple - How to save a photo:

- Open the text conversation in iMessages.

- Locate the image you want to save.

- Tap and hold the image until a menu appears.

- Tap Save. The image will be saved to your gallery within the phone's internal memory.

Android - How to send a photo:

- Open the Messaging application from the Home screen.

- Tap the new message icon, usually in the in the upper right corner.

- Tap the Attach button, which looks like a paperclip. Click on the "Pictures" option to add an existing photo, or take a new photo by tapping the "Capture Picture" icon.

- Tap "Send" when you're ready.

Android - How to save a photo:

- Open the Messaging application from the Home screen.

- Open the thread of messages that contain the photo.

- Tap and hold the photo until a menu appears.

- Select the "Save attachment" option from the menu.

- Select the checkbox next to the image.

- Select "Save." The image will be saved to the phone's internal memory.

The Best Way to Store Attachments

Saving images and videos locally to a device's internal memory can pose problems with most phones on the market today because they all have limited storage capabilities.

With continuing advancements in phone technology employing higher resolution front and rear cameras and shooting high-quality HD and 4K video, all of those selfies and photo memories can quickly make free space limited. Also, images only saved to a phone's local storage can easily be lost if the phone is accidentally damaged, misplaced, or stolen.

While it's always possible to transfer photos to a computer, there are other solutions to safely and securely save pictures to one place, that doesn't require you to plug in. That place is called the "Cloud."

Cloud accounts offer people a way to safely store photos in one place, whether they are from texting, email, Facebook, Instagram, or any other app. These accounts are also password protected, so your attachments are safe and secure.

Many cell phone carriers (Verizon, T-Mobile, AT&T, etc.) offer their customers a base-level "cloud storage" account for free. These accounts also have an automatic backup option that uploads and new photos, videos, or attachments that have been saved to your phone. The backup option settings can be adjusted to upload via WiFi only (recommended), and set to run hourly, daily, weekly, etc. Check with your specific carrier for specifications and how to log in but take advantage of this feature.

If this option is not available with your carrier, or you opt not to be tied with a specific provider, Google Photos, iCloud Photo Library, or Amazon Prime Photos may be great alternatives. These apps allow anyone with account access to upload photos and videos to a secured "cloud" account. These services offer free or low-cost unlimited storage for videos (up to 1080p) and pictures (up to 16-megapixels).

Uploading photos to a cloud account is the best way to backup and safely store your memories, and these photos will still be readily accessible to show and send to other friends and family.

How to Forward a Text Message

Whether it's a beautiful personal sentiment that you've received and want to share with a trusted friend or a chain message that you "must" send to 10 people within 1 hour or face dire consequences, there are times when you may want to forward a text message that you have received.

STEP BY STEP LESSON #3

These instructions will walk through how to forward a text message that you have received. Typically, text messaging applications will insert a "Fwd:" or "FW:" to indicate to the receiver that it is a forwarded message. These prefixes are removable and can be deleted if desired.

Apple - How to forward a text:

- Launch Messages from your Home screen.

- Tap and hold the message you'd like to forward.

- Tap More....

- Tap on the forward button in the lower right-hand corner, and a new message will populate, pre-filled with your forwarded text.

- Fill out the "To:" field with a contact's name or phone number.

- Edit the message as needed or write additional comments.

- Press Send and the message will be on its way.

Android - How to forward a text:

- Open the Messages application from the Home screen.

- Tap and hold on the message until a menu appears.

- Tap the Forward option from the menu, and a new message will populate, pre-filled with your forwarded text.

- Fill out the "To:" field with a contact's name or phone number.

- Edit the message as needed or write additional comments.

- Press Send and the message will be on its way.

How to Reply to Sender (instead of Reply All)

Messaging threads that contain multiple friends, co-workers, or family members are a great way to update a group of people at the same time. Sometimes however, it may not be necessary to reply to the entire group of people.

STEP BY STEP LESSON #4

These instructions explain how to reply to the sender of the original message, instead of responding to the whole group.

Apple - How to reply to sender-only, instead of reply all:

- Tap the "Messages" button at the top left of the iPhone Group MMS screen, which is displaying the group conversation you are reading. This will bring you back to the main "Messages" screen.

- Tap the icon to create a new message and enter the person's name you want to send a message to in the "To:" field.

- Enter your message text and tap "Send."

Android - How to set reply to sender-only, instead of reply all:

- Open the Messages app on the home screen.

- Tap More…

- Open the Settings.

- Tap the Advanced option.

- Tap Group messaging and then select Send an SMS reply to all recipients and get individual replies (mass text).

Android - To reply to sender-only in a current group message:

- Tap the group name(s) at the top of the screen to reveal all participants.

- Tap the chat icon next to a participant's name to message only that group member.

How to Schedule a Text to Send Later

This is one of my favourite features of texting applications. It's perfect for texting people in different time zones, setting up a personalized text to wish a friend a happy birthday while you're traveling, or sending good luck wishes to someone for an interview next Tuesday. Scheduling texts is an incredibly useful texting tool for multiple situations and scenarios.

The scheduling feature is also useful for messages that you may be unsure about sending, such as an emotional text message. It enables you to see how it feels typing out the text message and 'sending' it without really sending it. Typing out a text message like this, but then scheduling it for 4 or 6 hours later, provides a necessary time buffer to reflect and decide if the text message should really be sent. If you change your mind, just delete the scheduled message before it is actually sent.

STEP BY STEP LESSON #5

These instructions provide a walkthrough of how to delay sending a message and scheduling it to send minutes, hours, days, or weeks later.

Apple - Scheduling a text:

At the time of this writing, Apple does not provide a default way to schedule text messages on iPhone. However, there are several third-party options available in the App Store. Please refer to and review those texting apps, to select one that suits your needs.

Android - Scheduling a text:

- Open the Messaging application from the Home screen.

- Pick a recipient and type your message.

- Tap the three dots in the top right-hand corner.

- Select the "Schedule message" option from the menu.

- Pick a time and date for the message to send. Notice that the send button now has a small clock icon, which lets you know that it is set to send at a future time.

To review, edit, or cancel a scheduled message, press and hold on the message until a menu appears. The menu will contain various options allowing you to edit, cancel, or send now.

How to See if a Text was Delivered and Read

There are multiple ways to see if the text message you have sent to a receiver, has been delivered or read. The easiest and quickest way happens when both the sender and receiver are using the same messaging app with the same service carrier.

Whether it's an Apple product, Android, or another type of phone, status updates are nearly instantaneous in these cases.

STEP BY STEP LESSON #6

The instructions below explain how to view if a message was delivered, had any error messages, or was read by the receiver.

Apple - text message status reports:

- If the message has been sent via iMessage, it will be blue. If the receiver has the 'Send Read Receipts' option turned on, a delivery status will appear just underneath the message, saying Delivered or Read, with a date that the message was opened.

- If the message has not been sent via iMessage, it will be green and will not have the read/delivered receipt notifications available.

Android - text message status reports:

- Open the Messaging application from the Home screen.

- Select a text message and press and hold until a menu appears.

- Click on the "Message details" or "Message Info" option.

- Scroll within the details to find the "Status" which will give the current status of Sent, Delivered, or Failed. If there was an error when sending the message, a status code will be displayed.

To see if a message has been read, Android phones require the sender to enable a "Read Receipt" option within the texting application itself.

- Open the Messaging application from the Home screen.

- Tap More ...

- Tap the Settings option.

- Tap Chat settings.

- Locate the "Send read receipt" option and turn it on. When this setting is enabled, the receiver may be alerted upon opening the text message and given an option to send the 'read receipt' notice.

How and Why to Switch Between SMS and MMS

Short Messaging Service (SMS) and Multimedia Messaging Service (MMS) are terms frequently used when discussing texting jargon… here are the differences between them.

Most text messages are carried over SMS, which by design is low-priority. If network bandwidth is required for something considered to be higher priority - which includes all phone calls or an E911 search - providers can and do simply dump unsent SMS texts messages.

Like SMS, MMS messaging is a way to send a message from one mobile phone to another. The main difference is that MMS can include not just text, but also sound, images and video. MMS also does not impose the 160-character limit, so messages can be longer with a maximum size of 600kb, although carriers can impose their own size restrictions. Longer messages should always be sent via MMS or else the message is broken apart into multiple SMS messages that will arrive in a random order.

Based on the actual size, content, and length of your message, you may opt for one texting protocol over the other.

STEP BY STEP LESSON #6

The instructions below explain how to enable and switch between the MMS and SMS protocols.

Any Device - changing the text message protocol:

- Adding a "Subject" field to a text message will instantly convert a standard SMS text message to the MMS format, even if the subject content only contains a space. Check the texting app settings and options menus to add a subject line.

Apple - changing the text message protocol:

- Open the iMessage app from the home screen.

- Tap the Settings button.

- Scroll down to and tap Messages.

- Scroll down, then to enable, drag the MMS Messaging switch to ON.

- To disable, drag the MMS Messaging switch to OFF.

Android - changing the text message protocol:

- Open the Messaging application from the Home screen.

- Tap More ...

- Tap the Settings option.

- Tap Chat/Conversation settings.

- Locate the MMS options and enable as desired.

3

TEXT-IQUETTE

With the rise of texting communications, also comes a rise in the similarities and differences between people, common courtesies within various cultures, and lifestyle differences. There are many different sets of 'rules to live by' based on how you were raised, where you live, the type of occupation you have, and more.

Thankfully though, there are a few things that we all have in common, and as we traverse this communication phenomena known as texting, and whatever comes after texting, this chapter tries to identify and recognize these commonalities and apply them to the instant-messaging world via texting etiquette, or "text-iquette."

Text-iquette has been developed and based on two of the inherent traits that nearly every human being possesses. These two traits can be summarized as:

1. The innate need to communicate our thoughts, feelings, and ideas in hopes of building authentic connections with each other. This base need of genuine relationships is constant, whether the connection is formed as a friendship, familial, romantically or professionally based, or some other type.

2. The second trait is intertwined with the base desires to feel loved, heard, understood, and respected for who we truly are, to be loved and accepted, even when our thoughts, feelings, and ideas may not agree.

These traits are life-long internal instincts that fuel many of our daily actions, the words we speak, and the text messages we send.

Text-iquette can help build bridges across all of our differences and fuse kindness and common courtesy into the texting realm. It is based on these needs of self-expression, respect, and love, and lists *suggested* do's and don'ts for standards of etiquette for communication via text and instant-messaging.

The word *suggested* is used because in 90% of cases these are generally considered the right thing to do and best action to take. There are always exceptions to every rule which fall into the remaining 10%.

However, if you find yourself consistently in that other 10%, then the best rule of thumb for whether or not to send a text is asking yourself... *"Is this inappropriate in any way?"* Consider the receiver and place yourself in their shoes.

If you think it's inappropriate, it probably is a good idea to either wait and think about sending the text message later, or just not sending it at all. Proceed with caution in those circumstances and don't impulse text!

Schedules and Time Zones

Texting can connect people across a room or across the globe, in either case, it's important to respect and be mindful of the person's schedule and what time zone they are living in.

Even the best and most loving message is better received at the right time. Consider the following message:

> Hi gorgeous! I'm excited to see you tomorrow - we're going to have the *best* time and so much fun. :) I love you! xo

It's a beautiful expression of love and excitement at the thought of seeing your gorgeous face. Awwww :)

However, imagine if that text was sent at 7 AM EST to a receiver who lived in the DST time zone, where the local time was 1 AM, waking the receiver from a deep sleep and much needed rest after a long and exhausting day of work.

In this particular real-life scenario, the receiver read the message at 1:01 AM feeling slightly irritable from being woken up. They rolled over and fell back asleep, forgetting all about the lovely sentiments, because in the morning the message wasn't marked as "new" anymore.

The sender, not thinking of the time zone difference, wondered why the receiver hadn't answered. This resulted in hurt feelings and disappointment. Luckily the sender gently questioned the receiver later about why they hadn't responded, and the situation was resolved, but had the sender not expressed their feelings, this one texting interchange could have affected their whole relationship.

The same thing can happen for a busy day at work... whether it happens once or a hundred times, a message is glanced at, inadvertently forgotten about, and ill feelings may develop due to the initial unintended lack of respect for the receiver's schedule.

Text-iquette Tip #1:

Be mindful of and respect the receivers schedule and time zone. For help, see 'Scheduling a Text Message' in Texting Basics 101, and be sure and send text messages that will be sent and received at a convenient time for the receiver.

A case for the comma, period!

Languages have been developing for centuries and are ever-evolving and adjusting as societal norms fluctuate and influence the style of our communication. Punctuation hasn't fluctuated very much, however, and is still a necessary and consistent common practice in any and every language across the globe.

Capitalizing letters and using punctuation is crucial in helping the receiver understand what it is that you are trying to say. Using commas, periods, exclamation points, gives the receiver a better chance of understanding your intended meaning behind the text message and will result in fewer miscommunications. Consider the following text message and try to decipher the intended meaning behind the message:

> I want a man who knows what love is all about you are generous kind and thoughtful people not like you admit to being useless and inferior you have ruined me for other men I yearn for you I have no feelings whatsoever when we're apart I am so happy will you let me be yours

Because of the lack of any punctuation or capitalization, the text message is ambiguous and can be interpreted multiple ways, and perhaps not the way that the sender had intended. For every person that reads that text, it can convey a different meaning.

Read the same text message in versions #1 and #2 below. Both messages contain the exact same words, in the exact same order as the above message. However, notice how the entire meaning of the message changes based on slight differences in the capitalization and punctuation.

SAMPLE PUNCUATION 1

I want a man who knows what love is all about. You are generous, kind, and thoughtful. People not like you admit to being useless and inferior. You have ruined me for other men. I yearn for you. I have no feelings whatsoever when we're apart. I am so happy—will you let me be yours?

SAMPLE PUNCTUATION 2

I want a man who knows what love is. All about you are generous, kind, and thoughtful people, not like you. Admit to being useless and inferior. You have ruined me. For other men, I yearn. For you, I have no feelings whatsoever. When we're apart, I am so happy. Will you let me be? Yours,

The same text message with different capitalization and punctuation can have drastically different meanings. Imagine if the sender meant it the second way, and the receiver understood it to be the first way or visa versa?

The miscommunication and chaos created by the lack of commas is something easily avoidable.

Give your text receivers a better chance at understanding the intended meaning of your text messages, simply by using capital letters and punctuation.

Text-iquette Tip #2:

Punctuate your text messages and use capitalization where appropriate to avoid confusion over the intended meaning. Here are some basics to apply:

- End sentences with a period, question mark, or an exclamation point.
- Use commas to separate two clauses, as in the "Let's eat, Grandpa" example.
- Capitalize proper nouns, such as people's names, and specific places or things:
    - Bill took a ferry to see the Statue of Liberty, in NYC.
    - Bill took the Manhattan Ferry to see a famous statue.

Proofread Before Sending

There are whole websites dedicated to the funny and unfortunate mishaps of autocorrect, misspellings, and typos. Proofreading any messages, text or emails, letters, reports, documents - whatever it may be, proofread, proofread, proofread! It's easy to do and only takes about three extra seconds for a text. If you need a good laugh and a reminder to proofread your texts, visit the following websites:

- http://www.autocorrectfail.org

- http://www.damnyouautocorrect.com/

Here are fun examples of auto-correct texts messages:

Text-iquette Tip #3:

Before pressing the send button, re-read your text message and correct any misspellings and incorrect words.

Texting While Driving

Take a moment to run through the following exercise: Close your eyes and visualize yourself driving the length of an empty football field with your eyes closed. That might be doable, but still may not be a great idea.

Now picture yourself driving the length of the football field. Your eyes are still closed, except now the field has people on it... pedestrians pushing baby strollers, people walking dogs, skateboarders, bikers.

Add other cars on the field, moving towards you, moving with you and beside you.

Answering a text takes away your attention away from the road for about five seconds on average. Driving at 55 mph, that's enough time to travel the length of a football field. So while this notion of blindly driving down a football field filled with cars and pedestrians may seem crazy, it's unfortunately something that many drivers do every day.

The National Safety Council reported that in 2017, 1 out of every 4 car accidents in the United States is caused by texting and driving, totalling approximately 1.6 million crashes each year. Of those accidents, nearly 390,000 included fatalities or injuries.

Texting while driving is 6x more likely to cause an accident than driving drunk.

Law enforcement is also taking texting while driving very seriously. Cell phone use including texting while driving has been banned and is illegal in 47 states, carrying heavy fines and penalties for breaking the law.

The following table presents information based on the laws within each state, whether all cell phone use is banned for drivers, and the penalties and enforcements.

State	Hand-held Ban?	All cell phone use ban?	Texting ban?	Enforcements
AL	No	Drivers age 16 and 17 who have held an intermediate license for less than 6 months.	All drivers	Primary
AK	No	No	All drivers	Primary
AZ	No	School bus drivers; Learner's permit and provisional license holders during the first six months after licensing (effective 6/30/2018)	No	Primary: cell phone use by school bus drivers Secondary: cell phone use by young drivers (effective 6/30/2018)

AR	Drivers ages 18 to 20 years of age; school and highway work zones	School bus drivers, drivers younger than 18	All drivers	Primary: for texting by all drivers and cell phone use by school bus drivers. Secondary: for cell phone use by young drivers, drivers in school and work zones
CA	All drivers	School and transit bus drivers and drivers younger than 18	All drivers	Primary: handheld and texting by all drivers. Secondary: all cell phone use by young drivers.
CO	No	Drivers younger than 18	All drivers	Primary
CT	All drivers	Learner's permit holders, drivers younger than 18, and school bus drivers	All drivers	Primary
DE	All drivers	Learner's permit and intermediate license holders and school bus drivers	All drivers	Primary

DC	All drivers	School bus drivers and learner's permit holders	All drivers	Primary
FL	No	No	All drivers	Secondary
GA	Yes (eff. 7/1/18)	School bus drivers. Drivers younger than 18.	All drivers	Primary
HI	All Drivers	Drivers younger than 18	All Drivers	Primary
ID	No	No	All Drivers	Primary
IL	All Drivers	Learner's permit holders younger than 19, drivers younger than 19, and school bus drivers	All drivers	Primary
IN	No	Drivers under the age of 21.	All drivers	Primary
IA	No	Learner's permit and intermediate license holders	All drivers	Primary: for all offenses (effective July 1, 2017).

KS	No	Learner's permit and intermediate license holders	All drivers	Primary
KY	No	Drivers younger than 18, School Bus Drivers.	All drivers	Primary
LA	No	School bus drivers, learner's permit and intermediate license holders, drivers under age 18	All drivers	Primary
ME**	No	Learner's permit and intermediate license holders	All drivers	Primary
MD	All drivers, School Bus Drivers.	Learner's permit and intermediate license holders under 18. School bus drivers.	All drivers	Primary
MA	Local option	School bus drivers, passenger bus drivers, drivers younger than 18.	All drivers	Primary

MI	Local option	Level 1 or 2 license holders.	All drivers	Primary
MN	No	School bus drivers, learner's permit holders, and provisional license holders during the first 12 months after licensing	All drivers	Primary
MS	No	School bus drivers.	All drivers	Primary
MO	No	No	Drivers 21 years or younger.	Primary
MT	No	No	No	Not applicable
NE	No	Learner's permit and intermediate license holders younger than 18	All drivers	Secondary
NV	All drivers	No	All drivers	Primary
NH	Yes	Drivers younger than 18	All drivers	Primary

NJ	All drivers	School bus drivers, and learner's permit and intermediate license holders	All drivers	Primary
NM	Local option	Learner's permit and intermediate license holders.	All Drivers	Primary
NY	All drivers	No	All drivers	Primary
NC	No	Drivers younger than 18 and school bus drivers	All drivers	Primary
ND	No	Drivers younger than 18	All drivers	Primary
OH	Local option	Drivers younger than 18.	All drivers	Primary: for drivers younger than 18. Secondary: for texting by all drivers.

OK	Learner's permit and intermediate license holders, school bus drivers and public transit drivers	School Bus Drivers and Public Transit Drivers	All Drivers.	Primary
OR	All drivers	Drivers younger than 18	All drivers	Primary
PA	Local option	No	All drivers	Primary
Puerto Rico	All drivers		All drivers	Primary
RI	Yes	School bus drivers and drivers younger than 18	All drivers	Primary
SC	No	No	All drivers	Primary
SD	No	Learner's permit and intermediate license holders	All drivers	Secondary
TN	Drivers in marked school zones (effective 01/01/18)	School bus drivers, and learner's permit and intermediate license holders	All drivers	Primary

TX	Drivers in school crossing zones	Bus drivers. Drivers younger than 18	All drivers (effective 09/01/2017)	Primary
UT	See footnote*	Drivers under the age of 18.	All drivers	Primary for texting; secondary for talking on hand-held phone
VT	All drivers	Drivers younger than 18	All drivers	Primary
VA	No	Drivers younger than 18 and school bus drivers	All drivers	Primary: for texting by all drivers. Secondary: for drivers younger than 18.
WA	All drivers	Learner's permit and intermediate license holders.	All drivers	Primary
WV	All Drivers	Drivers younger than 18 who hold either a learner's permit or an intermediate license	All drivers	Primary

WI	No	Learner's permit or intermediate license holder	All drivers	Primary
WY	No	No	All drivers	Primary
Total	All drivers: 15 states and DC, Guam, and Puerto Rico.	School Bus drivers: 21 states and District of Columbia. Teen drivers: 38 states and District of Columbia.	All Drivers: 47 states, DC, Guam, and Puerto Rico.	Primary for all drivers texting: 43 states, DC and Puerto Rico. Secondary for all drivers texting: 4.

Source: Source Insurance Institute for Highway Safety 2017. Governor's Highway Safety Association.

*Utah considers speaking on a cell phone, without a hands-free device, to be an offense only if a driver is also committing some other moving violation (other than speeding).

** Maine has a law that makes driving while distracted a traffic infraction. 29-A M.R.S.A. Sec. 2118.

*** Listed as a part of contributing factors

Text-iquette Tip #4:

Do not text while driving! It's illegal plus no text message is worth risking your life, the lives of your passengers, and the lives of the other drivers.

Why Acronyms May Not Be a LOL Matter

NOTE: This subchapter applies to personal text messages between friends and family, as using acronyms is generally not recommended for business etiquette. Please reference the chapter on business texting etiquette for specifics on acronym usage professionally, when dealing with colleagues or clients.

Texting acronyms have taken on a language of their own, leaving newcomers to the texting arena at a loss for the meaning behind many of these abbreviated phrases.

As a sender, how do you decide when to use acronyms versus not? Aside from knowing the level of texting experience of the receiver, it's also important to consider their background, hobbies, occupation, and geographical locations. These factors all come into play with how a receiver may interpret what the acronym stands for because the context surrounding the acronym may not be apparent.

Texting acronyms, just like with any language, can have similar abbreviations that have very different meanings. In English, words that are spelled the same but have different meanings are called Homographs. For example, take the 3-letter word "bow." There are multiple different meanings to this word, and the reader must decipher the intended meaning based on the overall context of the sentence.

- bow (front of a boat)
- bow (at the waist)
- bow (tied with ribbon)
- bow (shoots arrows)

If there is any ambiguity in the message itself and the acronym could possibly be misinterpreted... it is highly recommended to spell out the original word or phrase.

Consider the common acronym LOL – many of us type this into a text and hopefully in context of the other 157 characters, the intended meaning of the acronym is accurately received. However, based on differences in location, occupation, hobbies, etc. that common LOL acronym can have nearly 100 different meanings! Can you guess which LOL meaning fits with the following text message?

> Hi! We saw the funniest thing on Bourbon Street today and thought of you :) Call me later and I'll tell you about it! LOL

In this simple example, LOL could easily be interpreted as laughing out loud, lots of love, Ladies of Louisiana, or lots of laughs. The following is a partial list of the meanings of LOL, to demonstrate the span of location references, business terms, religious meanings, and more.

Are there more LOL meanings that would fit with the above message? Read through and decide, you may be surprised!

Laugh(ing) Out Loud	Lots Of Love	League of Legends (gaming)	Little Old Lady
Loads of Love	Labor of Love	Lots Of Laughs	Land O' Lakes
Lots Of Luck	Loss of Life (insurance)	Locks of Love (charity)	List of Lists
Lack of Love (game)	Lowest of the Low	Lady of the Lake	Lots of Laughter
List of Links	Love of Life	Language of Love	Leg of Lamb
Land of Lincoln	Lord of Lords (Jesus)	Learn Online	Live-On-Line
Live Out Loud	Lightolier (Genlyte company)	Lord of Life (Church)	Laws of Life
Loss of Light	Lands of Lore (game)	Loyal Orange Lodge	Love On Line
Legend of Legaia (video game)	Living on Lipitor	Lots of Lag (online gaming)	Love Our Lord
Land of Love	Land of Legends (Canandaigua Speedway, NY)	Lack of Laughter (less common)	Log On Later
Language of Literature	Loss of Lock	Labels or Love (song by Fergie)	Lots of Lemons
Lots of Licking	Life of Loan	Life of the Land	Lots of Losers

	(banking)		(Rocket Arena 3 clan)
Load of Laughs	Limit of Liability (legal)	Lots of Lust	Lord Oh Lord
Lips on Lips	Lord of Lies (gaming)	Lots of Lollipops	Line of Learning (UK education)
Love Out Loud	Laughing On Line	League of Losers (chess team)	Loss of Load (transportation)
Ladies of Lousiana	Loser on Line	Living on Line	List Of Lights
Lords of Legend (gaming)	Lower Operating Limit (finance)	Length of Lease (realtors)	Love of Literacy (teaching)
Loss of Line (telephony)	Last or Least	Lewd Obscene Language	Leaning Over Laughing
Lot of Lamers	Lying Out Loud	Lawyers on Line	Limited Operational Life
Low Order Language	Limited Operation Life	Longitudinal Output Level	Lunatics on Line
Liar of Lies	League of Lightness (gaming clan)	Legend of Lothian (gaming)	Less Of Lip
Lovelock, Derby Field Airport, Nevada (IATA code)	Lying Online Laughter	Lord of the Lambs	Lord of Light

Text-iquette Tip #5:

Acronyms are fun and easy ways to express a wide range of phrases; however until there is a relationship established between the sender and receiver, it may be best to spell out the acronym.

Don't Send an Angry Text... Do This Instead!

It is human nature that when we are upset, there is a much higher chance of being overly emotional, irrational, and saying things we might regret later. When you are feeling angry, hurt, jealous, or upset for any reason, before hitting that send button, try the following tips.

5 Things to Do Before Sending an Impulsive Text:

1. Exercise: Go outside for a walk, a jog, do some yoga... do something to burn off excess energy.

2. Take deep breaths as follows:
   - Inhale slowly to the count of 4
   - Briefly pause holding your breath
   - Exhale slowly to the count of 4
   - Repeat 10x.
   - Optionally close your eyes during this exercise.

3. Draft a text message but don't send it. Write out all of your feelings. Refer to the Quips & Scripts chapters for ideas, if needed.

4. Try and distract yourself for 10-15 minutes or longer, then come back and reread your drafted text message.

Edit as necessary and allow 10 minutes before rereading. Repeat as needed.

5. Call a friend and confide how you're feeling to them. They may offer a different perspective and will have a more objective viewpoint.

After a cooling off period, you may come to find that the situation wasn't as drastic as you first thought, and that sending an outburst via text may create more havoc than working to resolve the issue.

If you're still angry or upset, refer to the Power of Words and Improving the Text within your Texts chapters. Realize the impact of what you might say and identify your goals and intentions before sending a message.

If your goal is to resolve the issue, at the end of the text message add a 'Call Me' or 'Get Together' text from the Quips & Scripts chapter to suggest talking over the phone or in person.

Remember the purpose of texting isn't for long conversations and complicated feelings, because of the pitfalls and miscommunications that can result from this type of text exchange.

> **Sample Conversation Template:**
>
> 1. Select a Text Opener. Example: "Hi, how are you?"
>
> 2. They may respond, but if they're also angry or hurt, they may not. Be Prepared.

> In either case, proceed to the next step.
>
> 3.   State texting goal, which is expression leading to a conversation.
>
> "<trait> is really important to me, and when <bad behavior>, it made me feel <upset/hurt/etc>. I don't want this to fester... are you around to chat?"

Sample Text Message:

> Loyalty is so important to me, and when I saw what happened, it upset me. I don't want this to fester... are you around to chat?

Text-iquette Tip #6:

It's best not to send a text message when emotionally charged and instead choose one or more of the activities above. After a cooling off period, discover your intention and goal, and draft a message that suggests talking or meeting in person.

Refer to the Improve the Text within your Text, and the Quips & Scripts chapters.

WHEN TO USE ALL CAPS

Using all capital letters has several use cases when writing a text message. However, it is generally recommended to avoid typing the whole text message in ALL CAPS, as receivers will often perceive the message as being yelled at and angry.

The sample text below is a mundane suggestion about dinner, but when typed in all capital letters it comes across more like a command rather than a suggestion.

Sample ALL CAPS text message 1: (BAD)

> LET'S GO OUT TO DINNER

An all-caps message can also be misleading and ambiguous because it's hard to discern acronyms and proper nouns.

Sample ALL CAPS text message 2: (BAD)

> THE VET BILL IS HERE

Does this message mean that wartime hero Bill came to visit, or that a bill from the veterinarian arrived in the mail?

Using capital letters within a text message can be an effective way to add emphasis to key words, however, depending on its usage can still be perceived as anger or have ambiguity.

For example, the text message below may lead one to think the sender has very strong feelings against potatoes.

Sample WORD CAPS text message:

> I don't feel like cooking
> POTATOES!

When using all capital letters to emphasize a word, be sure to select an appropriate word that conveys the intended meaning.

Sample WORD CAPS text messages:

> I'd absolutely LOVE to
> try that new restaurant :-)

> I'd absolutely love to try
> that NEW restaurant :-)

Capital letters can be used in combination within a text message to identify both acronyms and a word emphasized in all capital letters.

Bill took the ferry to see
the Statue of Liberty, in
NYC and got SEASICK!

I am SO TIRED of
pizza... NOT! lol

Text-iquette Tip #7:

Typing a whole sentence in capital letters is usually perceived as an angry message and can make it hard to distinguish acronyms and proper nouns. Instead, try to select keywords in the message for added emotional emphasis.

*%&$#!@ and Naked Pictures

There are times when many of us may be tempted to type a text message that contains profanity, whether it's common use in our everyday vocabulary, we're angry and making a point da**it, or just want to say F*** it! There may also be times when it seems like a good idea to send that suggestive image, in a virtual attempt to 'woo' the receiver with our au' natural beauty.

While fortunately or not, there are no image filters that autoscan texting photos, but mostly every smartphone manufactured today does have a built-in feature that limits and filters words that are considered to be modern-day swear words.

Any identified flagged words are automatically corrected, and the text message is sent as:

I ducking loved that movie!!! :-)

While some people, drunken sailors and the like, may find this profanity filter to be an annoyance, many state and federal governments have what is known as "Obscenity Laws."

Within the United States, the classification of "obscene" and thus illegal has been judged on printed text starting in 1897, which upheld a conviction for mailing and delivery of a newspaper which contained "obscene, lewd, lascivious, and indecent materials." This law was later upheld in several cases, including pictures and images considered as obscene, as recently as 2016.

There is no uniform national standard, so check with individual state obscenity laws before pressing that "Send" button.

Text-iquette Tip #8:

If you do decide to include profanity or naked photos as part of your text messages, be sure it's only to appropriate people.

And remember, once it's sent there is no going back. Your words and images are out of your control and will live on in the virtual world indefinitely.

Using Emoticons

NOTE: This subchapter applies to personal text messages between friends and family, as using emoticons are generally not recommended for business etiquette. Please reference the chapter on business texting etiquette for specifics on text messaging on a professional level when dealing with colleagues or clients.

Emoticons, or emojis, are fun ways to express and convey the intended meaning behind a text message. They are meant to mimic our facial expressions and can add a touch of character, fun, or spice to nearly any text message.

Consider the following messages and notice how different emoticons punctuate and influence the meaning. Write in the spaces provided, what you think the meaning is, and watch how the feelings change based on the emoticon used.

Sample Emoticon text messages:

I really like you 😊

I really like you 😑

I really like you 😍

> I really like you 😟
>
> I really like you 😄
>
> I really like you 😺

Emoticons can also be used as a fun way to tell a story within a text message. Here are some examples:

> **Sample Emoticon story messages with possible interpretations:**
>
>
> This couple is flying to NYC for some pizza.
>
> 🐚🔪⚽🏃😟
> Looks like someone is sad about a soccer game being rained out!

Text-iquette Tip #9:

Use emoticons to help show your intended meaning behind the text message and have fun with them.

One-Word Responses

There are times when one-word text messages may be appropriate. Perhaps there isn't much to say, you're busy, or other times when you are merely acknowledging the receipt of an earlier text message.

In general however, one-word messages may be perceived as low-interest and leave no room for conversation or connection to happen, especially if someone is sharing photos, sentiments, or feelings. Consider the separate text exchanges below.

Sample 1-word responses: (Bad)

One-word responses can also be inconsiderate if the receiver is on a limited monthly texting plan.

However through repeated use, one-word responses can be beneficially used to show a disinterest in someone you no longer wish to talk to, as the sender will see that you are not interested in engaging in conversation or building a connection. Eventually, the sender will get the message and quit initiating text conversations.

If you are looking to build connections with people, avoid repeatedly sending one-word responses.

Text-iquette Tip 10:

To build conversations and connections with people, avoid repeatedly sending one-word responses. Find a topic, something in common, or ask questions about the initial text message in order to carry the conversation. One-word responses are best used for simple acknowledgments or thank yous.

4

TEXTING AT WORK

Many corporations have started initiating texting protocols among their employees and staff, for multiple reasons, as more and more business communications are done via text. Questions arise like:

- When is it okay to text clients/patients/students?

- What information is appropriate to send via text messages?

- Can I use acronyms? Emoticons?

Improper use of texting, whether it is with colleagues or clients, can result in time-consuming and costly legal litigation. Misuse of acronyms, sharing private/inaccurate information, and general texting ambiguity can wreak havoc with business laws and ultimately damage your professional reputation and the reputation of the company.

If your organization does not currently have a texting policy in place, consider following these business texting tips and review the sample texting communication policy provided.

Keep in mind that texting in a professional business setting can be significantly different than a more relaxed and casual text conversation between friends. The suggested business etiquette rules below are slightly 'stricter' than the Text-iquette rules earlier.

Business Texting Etiquette

- **Elevate Communication Standards -** Every piece of communication is a reflection of your professionalism, including a text message. Save emoticons for your personal correspondence. Avoid abbreviations that can be confusing or ambiguous. Proofread and use punctuation.

- **Avoid Using Acronyms -** Every business has its own terminology and acronyms, so a term that is commonly used and obvious to you can easily be misinterpreted by clients, patients, or anyone outside of the organization. Misunderstanding acronyms can have devastating after effects including the possibility of the sender being held liable for negative results.

- **Limit Texting to Standard Work Hours** - Just like a late-night phone call from a family member in crisis, a late-night or off-hours text message signals an emergency. It's recommended to limit sending business-related text messages to near or within whatever the standard business hours are for the organization. If it is after-hours, wait until the next business day to relay your message or use a message scheduler to delay the sending time and date.

- **The Rule of Three** - If there are more than three separate questions in a response, either the initial text wasn't clearly stated or the receiver doesn't understand the task at hand. Complex subjects that require further explanation are best done via email or on the phone. Use the Call Me sample scripts to arrange a convenient time to talk and clear up any confusion.

- **Established Relationships Only -** Once you have been introduced, either virtually or in-person, ask what their preferred method of communication is and when possible, use that method whether it is texting, via phone, email, etc. Your first contact with a work colleague or client should never be a text, and afterward only used when there is an established business relationship.

- **Brevity is Soul of Wit -** It can be easy to send a rambling, lengthy text message, however, if the message is more than a few sentences, a phone call or email is most likely better. Depending on the carrier, and if the message type is SMS or MMS, longer messages can get broken apart and sent in random order. Keep it brief.

- **Don't Text Confidential Information -** Texting should never be used to relay any confidential or private information. As with other digital communication methods, the words typed and images that are sent can live on forever in a screenshot. Once you hit send, it's out of your control what the receiver chooses to do with that information.

- **Reply Promptly -** When you receive a message from a client or your boss, respond in a timely manner. Even if the response conveys that you need time to think about or research the subject. Be courteous and don't leave the sender of the message wondering and waiting for a response. It can create confusion and a lack of trust.

- **Look Up -** Constantly being on a mobile phone takes away from your professional image and can be distracting if someone is trying to have a conversation with you. Give your phone, laptop, and other electronic devices a rest so that you can be present, observe the environment and engage with others. At business lunches, put your phone away, and try an "Unplugged" meeting.

- **Sign off gracefully -** When the conversation is concluding, end the exchange with a thank you or a promise to follow up soon. Example closing scripts are within the Quips and Scripts chapter.

Sample Organization Texting Policy

The following sample is a list of texting communication standards that professional organization may wish to implement with their staff. Use this template as a starting basis to develop a texting communication policy that adheres to any specific business needs.

1. Text messages should only be sent to office associates within 1 hour of, or during standard business hours, unless if it is an emergency or otherwise stated as part of the job description.

2. Texting any private or confidential business-related information is prohibited.

3. When messaging clients, it is necessary to spell out any business acronyms to avoid confusion or misinterpretations. Do not use casual acronyms such as BRB, LMK, etc.

4. A text is a reflection of your professional image. Be professional and use complete words with punctuation. Do not use "u" for you. Use commas and periods to end sentences.

5. Reply within a reasonable time frame. Even a reply that you need additional time to gather information is sufficient.

6. If a message exchange goes beyond three responses and there are additional questions, set up a convenient time to talk via phone or meet, to remedy any confusion.

As with any corporate policy, have any Texting Communications Policy reviewed by Human Resources and Legal departments to ensure accordance with local, state, and federal laws.

5

AVOID TEXTING PITFALLS

Any form of electronic communication, whether it's emailing, texting, or instant-messaging... all share common pitfalls.

Humans for centuries have been developing their communication skills and improving the way we engage and interact with each other. Throughout time, we've naturally grown accustomed to understanding the meaning behind each other's facial expressions, hand gestures, and the tone of voice and inflection used when speaking.

In fact, the most classic communication studies, conducted by UCLA Professor Dr. Albert Mehrabian, found that only 7% of any message is conveyed through the actual words being used... only 7%!

The results concluded that 38% of communication is based on vocal elements, such as pitch and tone. The remaining 55% of the way humans interact is based on other nonverbal elements like facial expressions, gestures, posture, etc.

Texting and instant-messaging takes away 93% of the way humankind has learned to communicate and engage with each other.

Even a simple phrase like, "I'm okay," can be interpreted countless ways because we have none of the other communication aspects to go along with it.

So remember the next time you send or receive a text, it could be entirely misinterpreted without you even trying. Why?? Here are the most common texting pitfalls to be aware of in this brave new world of texting and electronic communication.

No Context in Texts

Context is defined as the circumstances and surroundings that form the setting for an event, statement, or idea, and in terms of which it can be fully expressed and understood.

In a chat or text message, you don't have the benefit of the context in which a message was sent, making it impossible to put ourselves in other person's shoes because we can't see those shoes.

There is no basis for understanding if any of the following circumstances apply:

- Is there a dog barking, child screaming, spouse questioning, or other possible distractions vying for their attention?

- Is the environment around them extremely noisy making it hard to concentrate?

- Is the sender at home, behind on a project and working late when they're supposed to be having dinner with family?

- Are they suffering from a cold? Maybe on cold medicine and not thinking with a clear head?

Any number of conditions or circumstances are possible, and we are completely unaware of any or all of them, which unfortunately leads to feeling less empathetic for the person on the other end of the line.

Some people are naturally more transparent about what's going on in their lives and may offer information about themselves or their lives, which makes it easier to get some context around text-based communications.

But even in those cases, the most transparent people with the most transparent messages still risk communication barriers and miscommunication without the full context of being in the same room.

Pitfall #1:
Without any context, it's hard to understand the other person's perspective. Ask questions and try putting yourself in their situation, then relate that to how you feel when interpreting text messages.

Missing Non-Verbal Cues

A person's body language, facial expressions, and tone of their voice all play a crucial part in how we understand what people are really trying to say. UCLA professor Albert Mehrabian has disseminated that further into the following categories:

- 55% of communication is through body language

- 38% through vocal tone, pitch, and emphasis

- 7% through the words and content of the message.

Based on this information, text conversations rely on just 7% of the way humankind has learned to communicate over the past centuries. There is no body language; you can't see facial expressions and reactions to your message, hear the tone of their voice or detect any other forms of nonverbal communication.

Without the benefit of nonverbal cues, there is a much higher risk of misinterpreting the intended meaning of the text message, and that's what communication is really all about – the intention behind your words, which are typically communicated in the other 93%.

Pitfall #2:
Because there's a high chance of misinterpreting the intended meaning of a text message, ask yourself... 'Are there other ways this could be read?'

Are We Engaged?

When you're having a face-to-face conversation with someone, it's easy to know if they are engaged in the discussion and you can gauge how they are interpreting your words. It's possible to notice that they respond better to quantitative information or grasp concepts better through a story or an anecdote.

These cues aren't available in texting, so there's no tailoring the conversation based on the other person's understanding, engagement, or comprehension. The lack of these engagement cues increases the odds of communication barriers and miscommunications in text messages.

In text-based communications, you may eventually learn each other's comprehension levels, communication styles and preferences, but it happens much slower, and there's far more time and trial-and-error involved.

Miscommunication in this instance is almost a necessity to learn that someone interprets a curt message as angry instead of merely written in a hurry.

Pitfall #3:
In texting, there's a higher learning curve when discovering

people's engagement level, communication styles and preferences but with time and patience, it is possible. Try each of the four texting styles in chapter 6 and see which style they respond the best too.

Naturally Detached

There's a certain level of detachment associated with sending messages through a phone or other device. The anonymity created by this feeling can lead to more conflicts because it's easier to confront/be rude/etc. to someone via text since you can't actually see them and see how your words are affecting them.

It becomes easier to let your emotional state color text messages when you can't see the look in someone's eyes. You're more likely to 'cross that line' that wouldn't normally be crossed if you were out to coffee with that same person.

Using this detachment and anonymity as a means to say things you wouldn't say otherwise isn't new. There are many examples throughout history of people hiding behind the veil of detached anonymity while criticizing other people, rulers, laws, and countries.

> *"In the early 1660s, in the reign of England's King Charles II, a printer called John Twyn was put to death for refusing to name the anonymous author of a piece that was critical of [the king]... Without it, we lose a valuable balance to the powers that be."*

– Brooke Magnanti, quoted in The Wall Street Journal.

In the United States, there are protections in place for what's called "reporter's privilege." This privilege protects a journalist who refuses to disclose a source, and it falls under the constitutional law because of this fact. People are less likely to confront others or disclose incriminating information when their name or face may be associated with the news or put their lives in jeopardy.

It's the same feeling of detachment and anonymity that is associated when sending text messages.

Pitfall #4:
Remember when texting, there is a person on the other end of the phone, who is very much a human being, with feelings and emotions. Any text message you send will affect them, their futures, their lives, and quite possibly the lives of those people surrounding them.

Being at Each Other's Text and Call

Having a mobile device gives people the perception that someone is always readily available – on any whim, beck or call, although logically we all know that's not the case.

Delays happen, and because text communications don't happen in real time, these delays have the potential to wreak havoc and create communication barriers.

There are two main types of delays in texting communications:

- Natural Delays: This is the natural timing of a response, which may be delayed due to a receiver's schedule and other issues pressing on their time.

- Latency: Latency is caused by technical glitches and delays when a text message is lost in the ether, or global network bandwidth is being reserved for higher priority communications.

NATURAL DELAYS

Despite best efforts by dating guides and other communication gurus, there is no standard protocol for when to or how quickly to respond. Should we be 'always' on and available at any time to respond to someone's texting whim? Are we expected to be each other's "Text and Call Girl/Guy"?

If receivers don't answer back as quickly as the sender expects or would like, they begin to wonder why they haven't responded. The sender may start to tell themselves a story that the receiver is ignoring them or mad at them.

Senders should consider that perhaps the receiver is in a meeting, driving, napping, having dinner with mom... or a host of other causes that don't produce the circumstances to send an immediate reply and cause natural delays to happen.

Adding to natural delays is the possibility for "latency," in which messages are sent and held or lost indefinitely, combined delays are a recipe for a miscommunication disaster.

LATENCY DELAYS

Sometimes text messages don't go through when they should for purely technical reasons… they're lost in the ether for a few hours, a day, even up to a week or longer. Latency happens, and it can be caused by a number of reasons including:

- **Location Issues**
  The location of the sender or receiver at the time a text message is sent may cause latency. If one of the mobile devices is located outside of network coverage, or where signals are weak or blocked, latency will occur. Even in areas with high coverage, latency can happen if a device is on the border between two coverage areas or traveling in a car above 35 mph and is changing coverage areas frequently.

- **Different Service Providers/Carriers**
  A sender and receiver on different cellular carriers may experience latency because of communication barriers between networks, or if the carrier prioritizes their own network traffic.

- **Network Traffic**
  Just like a busy highway, if there is heavy traffic on a network, the volume causes congestion catching

messages in a bottleneck which results in a latency delay.

- **Device Issues**

    If a device is turned off, obviously that will create a delay in the message delivery. However, devices with weak or uncharged batteries can also negatively impact delivery. Phone antennas within the device that have experienced damage due to being dropped, moisture, etc., are another possibility of why a particular device may experience latency delays.

- **There's a Glitch**

    Software bugs happen every minute of every day. Sometimes there may be a glitch in the phone's software, the software used to manage and transport communications, or any networking software that the message has to use along the route between sender and receiver.

- **Emergency Protocols**

    If there are local emergencies, a portion of network bandwidth is often reserved for crisis-response services, so that they have the best communication response times possible.

Delayed Responses - A Real Life Scenario

Consider the following situation that could commonly occur among friends, co-workers, clients or in dating. A sender initiates a text message to meet for a coffee.

> Hi! I'd love to grab a coffee with you later this week, if you're free? Let me know.

A latency delay occurs, and this message isn't received for four days. During that four-day time span, the sender questions if the receiver got the message and why they haven't responded. The sender may start feeling angry about being ignored, dejected, hurt, or any hosts of other emotions.

The receiver who was oblivious for those four days just received the message. They are excited at the aspect of meeting and in their mind are replying immediately with something like:

> A coffee would be great! What days/times/ work for you? :-)

The sender is completely unaware that the receiver just got the message, and potentially could act a little cold in their response if they text back immediately or the sender may choose to wait to respond.

The receiver, who was excited, is now left wondering why the sender is acting oddly after they just initiated an invite for a coffee.

Does this scenario ring any bells with your own texting experience?

Delays happen, whether natural or technical. In text-based communications, it may take seconds, minutes, hours, or longer for the other person to even receive your message.

Per an article in askmen.com, around .25-.5% of texts experience latency or don't go through at all. It sounds like a small percentage, but that's about one out of every 200 to 400 texts.

Below are the average number of texts that are sent out per day, according to age. For the typical adult under the age of 45, that equates to about one text message every three days.

AGE	# AVG. DAILY TEXT
18-24	128
25-34	75
35-44	52
45-54	33
55+	16

This inadvertent delay may cause a total misunderstanding between the sender and receiver, for absolutely no reason at all.

Pitfall #5:
Latency and natural delays happen... be patient. Check the message status and details for any errors. If you are unsure, resend the original message to gain peace of mind.

Difficulty Staying on One Topic

Texting can lead senders to ask a variety of questions or discuss multiple topics within a single text message, which can lead to several communication issues. Consider the following messages:

> Hi! How are you? I just scored some amazing seats for that show on Saturday - are you still able to go? Maybe we could grab a drink or dinner beforehand too. :)

> I'm good! Saturday sounds fun... count me in. What time?

This might be a semi-typical text message exchange, and it seems like a pleasant conversation. However, when we inspect it more closely, there are multiple topics the receiver could have responded to and several instances where a potential loss of relationship-building connection could have happened.

The table below highlights the various topics in the first text initiated by the sender and possible responses that the receiver may have been able to express or share, had they been given the opportunity.

TEXT TOPICS	POSSIBLE RESPONSE
Hi! How are you?	Comments on day/mood/overall feeling - big meeting at work, excitement on a new project, etc.
I just scored amazing seats for the show on Saturday!	Excitement or apathy regarding the performance, discussions about their love of the venue and the last trip there, reminiscing about the decade-old collection of the performer's t-shirts.
Are you around to go?	Availability of weekend schedule and other fun events going on in their life that they may want to share.
We could grab a drink or dinner beforehand too	Discussion of food and restaurants, where to go.

The communication issues that arise from sending a text with multiple topics are listed below.

- **One Topic Response**
  Sending a text message containing multiple topics makes it difficult for the receiver to address each point individually, and they're more likely to respond to the whole stream of messages with one blanket reply, rather than addressing each individual topic, as was the case in this example.

- **Missed Opportunities to Build Connection**
  The receiver must decide which topics to respond to and leave out much of the possible conversational

responses that help build the connection between two people. In this example, the topics were fairly easy. Although there were plenty of missed opportunities to develop a deeper connection and relationship.

- **Selective Responding**
  Receivers will be naturally selective and respond to some topics while ignoring others. Whether or not the receiver is aware of this or doing it unintentionally, this behavior can leave the sender feeling unheard if the ignored topics are important to them. If the receiver is intentionally being selective and not responding to certain subjects, they may also experience an uneasy feeling about the topics that go unaddressed.

Pitfall #6:
When sending texts, stay on one topic at a time and give the receiver a chance to respond to that topic before starting a new topic.

Distractions Happen

That old saying "When it rains it pours" comes to mind for this particular pitfall. The phone can ring, doorbell ding, a child can sing... any number of distractions can happen during a text conversation.

With texting, it's also easy to have multiple conversations going simultaneously with various people, and unfortunately, multitasking isn't a skill that everyone has mastered.

These distractions, whether from the environment or a swarm of other message threads, lead to less connection with one particular text conversation and therefore less connection with the sender(s).

Distractions and multiple messages may also create a sense of feeling bombarded, overwhelmed, and lead to less concentration efforts available to engage in conversation.

If you can't give a message your full attention or a prompt response, reply with one of the following messages:

> Hi! I'm tied up right now but will get back to you [later today, tomorrow, in an hour, etc.]

> Sorry currently swamped!! Are you around later to catch up?

> Hey - busy atm. I'll msg you in a bit.

The only caveat is, if and when you tell someone you'll respond later, make sure to follow through and get back to them. Otherwise, the receiver will start to lose trust over time not only with those "I can't respond right now" messages, but everything you say may mean less because they're not sure if you value them or your relationship/friendship enough to follow through with what you say.

Pitfall #7:
During busy times, either wait to respond due to the natural delays that occur in life, or send a short reply and follow up later.

6

DISCOVER YOUR
TEXTING PERSONALITY

Communication is one of the keys to success in any relationship, whether your texting with your friends, mom, co-workers, boyfriends, girlfriends, or other family members.

Each one of us is unique. No one else comes at life with our perceptions, experiences, culture, or beliefs. No one else was raised in your country, in the same state, on the same street, went to the same schools and had the same teachers, was raised with the same family, and experienced and perceived the exact same things as you have. So no one will text and communicate ideas in the same way as you will.

How you text and communicate has a major impact on how others see you, how effectively you're able to deal and interact with others, and manage people and projects, personally and professionally.

While all of these characteristics and traits certainly add to your personal communication style, studies have shown there are four major styles of communicating, which have been adapted to fit the texting and instant-messaging world.

The Four Texting Personalities

It is widely accepted that there are four main styles of communication. When applied to texting we'll call these styles:

- Executive

- Entertainer

- Scientist

- Comforter

The original communication styles were developed from long-standing theories of human interaction based upon the Greek physician Hippocrates (ca. 460 BCE–370 BCE) who is often credited with developing the theory of the "four humors."

Hippocrates theorized that there are four fundamental bodily humors which significantly influence the body and its emotions. Each humor is correlated with a primary color, and natural element that exhibit similar characteristics. The four humors are:

- **Blood**: Red, Air.
- **Yellow bile**: Yellow, Fire.
- **Black bile**: Black, Earth.
- **Phlegm**: Blue, Water.

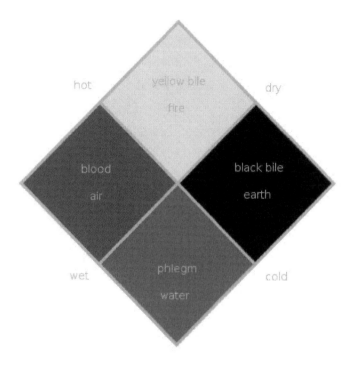

After further research and investigation each humor or temperament, as they were later known, came to be associated with specific physiological and emotional traits.

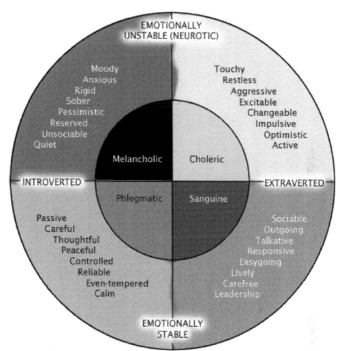

Eysenck, H.J and Eysenck, M.W. *Personality and Individual Differences.*
Plenum Publishing, 1958.

Hippocrates' theories were later combined with Carl Jung's research to create the current communication styles and personality traits associated with them. Through additional research, these styles have been tweaked to fit the modern-day era of electronic communications.

Take time and read through each texting type and the attributes associated with that communication style. Most people will identify with one or more of them, having a primary and secondary style. It's also possible to decipher which texting style certain people in your life are and enable you to respond accordingly for enhanced text conversations.

THE EXECUTIVE

- Likes being in control and at the top
- Values getting things done
- Decisive and often a risk-taker
- Good at delegating tasks to other people
- Can be private about personal matters
- Strong conversationalist
- Likes to be where the action is
- Competitive, enterprising, efficient
- Fearless; no obstacle is too big to tackle
- Results-oriented and driven

THE ENTERTAINER

- A social butterfly who likes being the center of attention
- Values enjoyment in life and helps others to do the same
- Full of ideas and impulsive in trying them
- Wants work to be fun for everyone
- Talkative and open about self; asks others' opinions
- Can be extroverted
- Flexible; easily bored with routine
- Intuitive, creative, spontaneous, flamboyant approach
- Optimist; nothing is beyond hope
- Celebration-oriented

THE SCIENTIST

- Has an analytical mind
- Values accurate information
- Plans everything thoroughly before deciding
- Prefers to work alone
- Can be introverted
- Quick to think but slow to speak
- Organized; cautious, logical, thrifty approach
- Problem solver
- Detailed and Idea-oriented

THE COMFORTER

- Enjoys harmony and avoids conflicts
- Values being accepted by others
- Prefers stability in circumstances
- Slower with major decisions; dislikes change
- Builds strong networks of friends
- Good listener; can be timid about voicing contrary opinions
- Concerned for others' feelings; can be a people pleaser
- Easy-going; likes slow, steady pace
- Friendly & sensitive; no person is unlovable
- Relationship-oriented

QUIZ: Find Your Texting Personality

Understanding your own texting communication style is crucial, as it will give insight into your interactions, relationships, and overall communications with others.

This is an informal survey consisting of 18 questions that are designed to determine how you usually act in everyday situations, and will help to get a clear description of how you see yourself.

TEST QUESTIONS

Circle A or B in each pair of the following statements, by choosing which statement is the one that accurately describes you the majority of time. There are no right or wrong answers. Think through each question and be honest with yourself and the answers you choose.

1.　　**A)** I'm usually open to getting to know people personally and establishing relationships with them.
B) I'm not usually open to getting to know people personally and establishing relationships with them.

2.　　**A)** I usually react slowly and deliberately.
B) I usually react quickly and spontaneously.

3.　　**A)** I'm usually guarded about other people's use of my time.
B) I'm usually open to other people's use of my time.

4.   **A)** I usually introduce myself at social gatherings.
        B) I usually wait for others to introduce themselves to me at social gatherings.

5.   **A)** I usually focus my conversations on the interests of the people involved, even if that means straying from the business or subject at hand.
        B) I usually focus my conversations on the tasks, issues, business, or subject at hand.

6.   **A)** I'm usually not assertive, and I can be patient with a slow pace.
        B) I'm usually assertive, and at times I can be impatient with a slow pace.

7.   **A)** I usually make decisions based on facts or evidence.
        B) I usually make decisions based on feelings, experiences or relationships.

8.   **A)** I usually contribute frequently to group conversations.
        B) I usually contribute infrequently to group conversations.

9.   **A)** I usually prefer to work with and through others, providing support when possible.
        B) I usually prefer to work independently or dictate the conditions in terms of how others are involved.

10.   **A)** I usually ask questions or speak tentatively and indirectly.
        B) I usually make empathic statements or directly expressed opinions.

11.   **A)** I usually focus primarily on ideas, concepts, or results.
        B) I usually focus primarily on persons, interactions, and feelings.

12.   **A)** I usually use gestures, facial expression, and voice intonations to emphasize points.
        B) I usually do not use gestures, facial expressions, and voice intonations to emphasize points.

13.   **A)** I usually accept others' points of view (ideas, feelings, and concerns).
        B) I usually don't accept others' points of view (ideas, feelings, and concerns).

14.   **A)** I usually respond to risk and change in a cautious or predictable manner.
        B) I usually respond to risk and change in dynamic or unpredictable manner.

15.   **A)** I usually prefer to keep personal feelings and thoughts private, sharing only when I wish to do to.
        B) I usually find it natural and easy to share and discuss my feelings with others.

16.   **A)** I usually seek out new or different experiences and situations.
        B) I usually choose known or similar situations and relationships.

17.   **A)** I'm usually responsive to others' agendas, interests, and concerns.
        B) I'm usually directed toward my own agendas, interests and concerns.

18. **A)** I usually respond to conflict slowly and indirectly.
     B) I usually respond to conflict quickly and directly.

Quiz questions were taken from The Platinum Rule by Tony Alessandra, Ph.D, &
Michael J. O'Connor Ph.D. New York, New York, Warner Brooks 1996

HOW TO SCORE THE TEST

Circle your answers in the table below, then count the
numbers of items circled in each column. Total each column,
and write the answer in the space provided.

	O	G	D	I
	1A	1B	2B	2 A
	3B	3A	4A	4B
	5A	5B	6B	6A
	7B	7A	8A	8B
	9A	9B	10B	10A
	11B	11A	12A	12B
	13A	13B	14B	14A
	15B	15A	16A	16B
	17A	17B	18B	18A
Column Totals:				

DETERMINING YOUR TEXTING STYLE

Compare the "O" column with the "G" column and circle the letter that has the highest total.

Compare the "D" column with the "I" column and circle the letter that has the highest total.

If you circled the G and D, you tend towards the Executive texting style.

If you circled the O and D, you show many qualities of being an Entertainer.

If you circled the O and I, you're predominantly a Comforter.

If you circled the G and I, you have lots of Scientist characteristics.

Communicating Tips for Each Texting Style

The following provides an overall description of each texting style, typical personality, and behaviour traits, and tips on how to interact and communicate with each one.

While these guidelines may be useful, it's important to remember that everyone has primary and secondary texting styles that they can and will traverse between.

THE EXECUTIVE

This communication style is driven by two things: the need to get things done and the desire to be in control. They are comfortable in settings where they can help manage people and take control of situations.

Fast-paced and goal-oriented, Executives are focused on bottom-line results and achieving success. This go-getter mentality makes them innate leaders, but it also means they can come across as impatient and insensitive.

Text traits of an Executive:

- Little to no use of emoticons
- Text length tends to be shorter, under 100 characters
- Conversations are direct and goal-oriented
- May often send one-word responses

Text Tips for Executives:

1. Ask follow-up questions to text you receive, as a way to connect with people.

2. Realize with texting there doesn't need to be a goal.

3. Add some fun to your text life with jokes or giphys.

4. It's okay to... *feel*.

How to Text an Executive:

5. Be clear, brief, and precise.

6. Be well-prepared to provide solutions to problems.

7. Keep small talk to a minimum

8. Stick to the goal and key points.

9. Avoid too much detail.

10. Find out their goals and provide options, clearly stating costs and benefits.

11. Supply concrete data to back up claims of progress.

THE ENTERTAINER

Most people love entertainers. They are usually fun to be around, always trying to make others laugh, and they thrive on being the center of attention. They are engaging, charismatic and energetic, and like being where the action is. They are optimists who are good at selling others on their vision and goals.

Although their enthusiasm and charm make them influential people, they can sometimes be impulsive decision-makers who take risks without checking the facts first. They listen to their intuition—which can be a good thing—and what their "gut" is telling them. They may have shorter attention spans and can find it hard to be alone.

Text traits of an Entertainer:

*   May have moderate to high use of emoticons

- Text length may be endless... multiple streaming texts are common
- Conversations are typically fun-oriented
- May have multiple subjects in the same texts

Text Tips for Entertainers:

1. Ask questions and be sure to include peoples' ideas and opinions in conversations.

2. Remember to be and express yourself authentically.

3. Connect with yourself more and the intentions of your messages.

4. It's okay to... *not always be 'on'*.

How to text with an Entertainer:

1. Take time to socialize with them.

2. Create fun, lively atmospheres that have new and diverse elements.

3. Help them prioritize.

4. Try to skip unimportant details and dull material.

5. After a meeting, be clear about who is going to do what and by when.

6. Help make them feel good about themselves and look great in front of other people.

7. Be slow to criticize them.

8. Motivate them with praise.

THE SCIENTIST

This communication style is very analytical and geared toward problem-solving. Methodical and detail-oriented, Scientists are usually slow decision-makers that are very deliberate about the choices they make. Before making a decision, they weigh the pros and cons and look at problems from every possible angle.

Their high expectations can make them come across as overly critical and pessimistic. They are perfectionists by nature and can quickly fall into the trap of "analysis paralysis," repeatedly analyzing the same situation. Leaning towards the skeptical side, they may prefer to see promises in writing.

Texts traits of a Scientist:

- Little to Moderate use of emoticons
- Text length typically is just under the 160-character limit, will send additional text but only if necessary
- Conversations are purposeful, often with questions for more data

Text Tips for Scientists:

1. Ask questions about a person's thoughts and feelings, not always just for information.

2. Try using a wide variety of words to add some spice to your messages.

3. Remember to connect with your feelings.

4. It's okay to... *add fun and emotions.*

How to Text with a Scientist:

5. Avoid too much small talk and socializing.

6. Give them space to think things through.

7. Be prepared to answer any questions thoroughly with precise data.

8. Make good on your promises and follow through.

COMFORTER

Of the four texting styles, this one is the most people-oriented. Comforters are warm, nurturing individuals who value interpersonal relationships above all other things. They tend to be very loyal employees, devoted friends, and excellent team players.

Peacemakers by nature, they often avoid conflicts and confrontations. They are always striving to build strong networks of friends and open to sharing their lives and responsibilities with others. Like Scientists, they can be thorough planners and risk-averse. They value consistency, authenticity, and sincerity.

Texts traits of a Comforter:

- Moderate use of carefully selected emoticons
- Text length typically is around the 160 character limit, will possibly send additional texts if they feel it's okay
- Conversations are caring-oriented and nurturing

Text Tips for Comforters:

1. Ask questions to gauge others' opinions before raising new ideas to help ease conflicts.

2. Try to be clear with your intentions and goals.

3. Realize it's okay to... *speak your mind and be different.*

How to Text a Comforter:

4. Be patient and show genuine interest in them as a person.

5. Build a relationship with them.

6. Learn about their personal lives before getting down to business.

7. Reduce fears over changes by clearly explaining the benefits to them and those around them.

8. Be predictable and consistent.

9. Follow through with stated promises.

10. Focus on their feelings. Be warm and inviting.

11. Don't push them into a corner to get what you need.

7

IMPROVING THE SUBTEXT OF YOUR TEXTS

Many instant-messaging and texts misinterpretations happen because we doubt the sender's intentions. It's very easy to read into a text message – even beyond what the intentions of that message initially were.

That's human nature; to try to create context where it doesn't exist, and to fit the puzzle pieces of life together into some recognizable pattern. Even more so, studies have shown that human nature may tend to lean towards the negative side when creating that context.

Management scholar Kristin Byron believes that misinterpretation comes in two forms: neutral or negative. Messages that were originally intended to be positive are perceived by the receiver in a neutral way, and messages with intentions that aren't clear tend to be viewed more negatively. While this tainted perception might be human nature, as receivers, we do have some control over it by consciously deciding to give message senders the benefit of the doubt. Assume the sender was happy when sending the message, and it may save a lot of grief.

What about as a sender? After reviewing the pitfalls of texting chapter, and discovering your texting style and the styles of your closest compadres, how can we best convey our thoughts, feelings, ideas, and emotions via text, so that they are received in a neutral or positive way?

There are three ways: Realize the power behind your words and the influence they can have, Discover your true intentions, and Define a Texting Goal.

The Power Behind Words

Words are SO incredibly powerful. Each text you send will have one of two possible outcomes; having either a positive effect or a negative effect on the receiver. Words can be and have been used throughout history as a means to build each other up or tear each other down.

Just becoming conscious and aware of the power behind our words is an excellent start, and this cognition will start influencing the manner of your interactions.

"Words are singularly the most powerful force available to humanity. We can choose to use this force constructively with words of encouragement, or destructively using words of despair. Words have energy and power with the ability to help, to heal, to hinder, to hurt, to harm, to humiliate and to humble." ~Yehuda Berg

Whether we are texting or speaking, it's important to be mindful of the outcome our words will have. Our texts to someone can affect their whole day, week, or even their whole life, depending on the level in which it was received.

If our words and intentions are based negatively, they will in turn have a negative impact. The receiver will feel worse, the relationship will be lessened, and we reduce the ability to restore a connection to a place of love.

If our words and intentions are based positively, with a feeling of supportiveness and sincere good will, they will in turn produce a positive impact. The receiver will feel better upon reading the message, the relationship will be improved, and we increase the connection with that receiver.

Take a moment and complete the following exercise:

1. Think back to a really happy time in life... maybe a celebration, wedding, graduation, birth of a child, or an accomplishment. Visualize the details of that memory and put yourself in that moment. Do you remember what was said? Do you remember what you felt? In the space provided, write down key things that were said and how you felt in that moment.

_____

_____

_____

_____

2. Now think back to a time when you were sad... perhaps grieving a loss, during an argument, or a time when you felt betrayed, disappointed, or hurt. In the space provided, write down the key phrases that really affected you in that moment.

_____

_____

_____

_____

Discovering Your Intentions

So words are powerful... yes, but really what are words? Words are just a random combination of letters that are assigned a meaning based on the current culture and location. On a deeper level however:

Words are the symbols used in modern communication to express our intentions and desires.

And that's what communication is really all about – the intention behind the words.

Intentions are the subconscious base-level thoughts and beliefs and that drive the everyday conscious thoughts behind our words and ultimately our text messages. There are two kinds of 'intentions,' which we'll categorize into good intentions and bad intentions.

Good intentions are thoughts that will make you and the receiver of your text message feel good. Good intentions evoke feelings of any of the following:

Love	Joy	Generosity
Happiness	Hopefulness	Connectedness
Contentment	Self-Worth	
Peace	Elation	Confidence

Bad intentions are any thoughts that feel produce a sense of heaviness. These may evoke feelings of any combination of the following:

Sadness	Guilt	Anger
Fear	Resentment	Bitterness
Betrayal	Low self-esteem	Regret
Despair	Worthlessness	Apathy

How do you know what your intention is? Take a look at how you feel about the person or situation in question. Be honest, and ask yourself the following questions:

- Are you sending the text message from a place of peace/joy/love?   Or   from   a   place   of sadness/anger/fear?
- Does thinking about sending this message make you feel lighter and happy? How do you think the receiver feel?
- Do you want to benefit or sincerely help the receiver in some way?
- How can you help or improve in this situation?

Even difficult texting conversations, ones that are awkward and slightly uncomfortable, can be sent with good intentions. Text messages sent with good intentions are received and interpreted better.

The energy we put into the world matters, even the intentions behind a 160-character text message. Energy matters.

There are a million analogies for mind over matter, as a man thinketh so is he, and even scientific studies that show how our intangible thoughts become tangible matter as we think something and different parts of our brains light up with activity. That is our thoughts taking form and moving from the intangible to the tangible! Thoughts produce things.

When we think thoughts filled with positivity it is proven to have beneficial effects on our bodies... emotionally, physically, and spiritually. And likewise with negative thoughts... they produce negative results.

What is the Texting Goal?

Lastly, improving the text within our texts is also influenced by our goal. What is the ultimate outcome you are trying to produce or accomplish?

Craft the words of your text messages based on your intentions and goals. Below is a sample texting template with a clear goal in mind.

General Texting Template:

1. Send an 'Opener' text.
2. <Response>
3. Texting Goal "So I just heard about... " etc.
4. <Response>
5. Send a 'Get Together' or 'Call Me' text.
6. <Response>
7. Send a 'Closer' text.

8

TEXT QUIPS AND SCRIPTS

Quips and Scripts is a reference guide of a plethora of sample texting scripts and templates that can be used in multiple situations and scenarios.

You can refer to this section as often as needed for new ideas on ways to say old things, spice up your daily texting life, and learn how to express difficult or complicated thoughts and feelings in positive ways.

The start of each section has a texting template that can be used as the basis to create a conversation. This template can be your guide at first, and as you become more comfortable, you will naturally develop more personalized conversational templates.

100 Ways to Say Hello

Most people appreciate the gesture of saying a hello because it let's them know they've crossed your mind and that's a compliment!

Use these conversation starters as the basis to open up the lines of communication between you and a message receiver. To choose the best hello, think of the intended receiver and picture their face, feel your intent, and scan through the sample scripts to find an opener text message that resonates with you.

There are casual 'whaddup' hellos, reaching back out to you because it's been awhile hellos, professional, flirty, and every type of hello in between.

HOW TO RESPOND TO AN OPENER

Connections begin with conversations, and conversations begin with an opener. In order to build better connections, it's imperative to be a better conversationalist. Whether you are sending an opener text message or have received one, people use these as a polite way to strike up and carry on conversations.

In either case, it's always good to be ready with possible opener responses so that when you are asked 'How are you?,' the conversation can carry on smoothly and it doesn't get potentially awkward like the following one.

> Hi! How are you?

> Hey :) I'm great thanks! How are you?

> Doing good :)

> What's new?

> Oh not much. You?

> Same old, same old.

While it's polite and friendly, the conversation can easily stall here, unless someone asks another opening question.

When someone asks you an opener question, use that opportunity to talk about something that is really exciting you at the moment. People love passion and excitement - it's contagious!

Each day, mentally prepare a few possible responses for openers based on what is going on in your life that is exciting. These options will be different for every individual on any given day, and while life may not always be fireworks, find your passion and share it. Topic suggestions may include:

- New TV show or movie you've watched
- A class, workshop, party, show or event you've attended
- Loving that latest best seller? Share it!
- Recent vacation or new trip coming up.

> Hi! How are you?

>> Hey! I'm doing great, thanks :) I just took a Thai cooking class on the Westside - it was SO fun!

This response gives the sender multiple threads of possible conversational topics to strike up such as:

- Where did you take the class?
- Share a recent experience with Thai food.
- What inspired you to sign up?
- What recipes did you learn to make?
- Any leftovers to share?
- Are you taking more classes? I'd love to try one sometime.

Some people aren't great conversationalist, so if there isn't a response or they send a one-word response, follow up with a related question to carry the conversation.

Sounds fun!

Do you like Thai food? What's your favorite dish?

Building connection through conversations starts with an opener, and sharing what you are feeling passionate about that day in responses. Look for possible topic threads about the other person, get them talking more about their passions, interests, and lives, and you'll quickly start building better connections.

'Opener' Template:

1. Send an opener: "hi!"
2. Response of: "Hi. How are you?" or sometimes just even a "Hello".
3. Share what you are feeling passionate or excited about and give them possible topics to carry on the conversation. If the conversation lulls, ask them if they've read/watched/been to whatever it is you've just done and what they thought of it.

OPENER QUIPS & SCRIPTS
Use the checkboxes to track which openers are your favourites
or that you've used.

- ☐ Hi!
- ☐ Howdy!
- ☐ G'day to you *hat tip*
- ☐ Breaker breaker 1 9, do you copy?
- ☐ Guten Tag!
- ☐ Hey
- ☐ Hello 😊
- ☐ What's shakin'?
- ☐ How's it going?
- ☐ Heyyyyyy!
- ☐ Howdy cowboy ;)
- ☐ Hiya handsome/beautiful
- ☐ Hey sexy!
- ☐ Namaste <3
- ☐ What's happening hot stuff?
- ☐ Hey I haven't heard from you lately. How are you?
- ☐ Hey - you've been MIA lately... everything okay?
- ☐ Long time no talk stranger! :)
- ☐ Hi :) I was just thinking about you... how have you been?
- ☐ Hey! I'm sorry we've lost touch... how are you?
- ☐ You've crossed my mind lately and I just wanted to say hi :)

- ☐ Hello gorgeous x

- ☐ I'm sorry I haven't been better about texting… that doesn't mean I haven't been thinking of you though. How are you?

- ☐ Been swamped lately, but catching a breather and wanted to give you a shout hellllloooooooooo!

- ☐ Sorry for the late reply - work has been crazzzzy!

- ☐ Hello, sunshine!

- ☐ Howdy, partner!

- ☐ Hey, howdy, hi!

- ☐ What's kickin', little chicken?

- ☐ Peek-a-boo!

- ☐ Howdy-doody!

- ☐ Hey there, freshman! <sophomore/junior/senior>

- ☐ Hi, mister!

- ☐ I come in peace 👽

- ☐ Put that cookie down!

- ☐ Ahoy, matey!

- ☐ Hiya!

- ☐ 'Ello, gov'nor!

- ☐ Cherrio luv!

- ☐ Top of the mornin' to ya!

- ☐ What's crackin'?

- ☐ GOOOOOD MORNING, <CITY>!

- ☐ 'Sup, homeslice?

- ☐ Howdy, howdy, howdy!

- ☐ Hi Batman.
- ☐ Here's Johnny!
- ☐ You know who this is?
- ☐ Ghostbusters, what'd ya want?
- ☐ Yo!
- ☐ Whaddup buttercup
- ☐ Greetings and salutations!
- ☐ 'Ello, mate.
- ☐ Heeey, baaaaaby
- ☐ Hi, muffincake!
- ☐ Yoooouhoooo!
- ☐ How you doin'?
- ☐ I miss your face.
- ☐ What's cookin', good lookin'?
- ☐ Howdy, miss.
- ☐ Why, hello there!
- ☐ Hey, boo.
- ☐ Jambo (Swahili)
- ☐ Bonjour (French)
- ☐ Hallo (Afrikaans)
- ☐ Nín hǎo (Chinese)
- ☐ Hei (Finnish)
- ☐ Annyeonghaseyo (Korean)
- ☐ Ahoj (Czech)
- ☐ Kon'nichiwa (Japanese)

- ☐ Moshi moshi (Japanese)
- ☐ Zdravo (Slovanian)
- ☐ Labas (Lithuanian)
- ☐ Merhaba (Turkish)
- ☐ Olá (Portugese)
- ☐ Helo (Welsh)
- ☐ Ahoy (Pirate)
- ☐ Alo (Romanian)
- ☐ Hej (Danish)
- ☐ Dia duit (Irish)
- ☐ Halló (Icelandic)
- ☐ G'Day Mate (Aussie)
- ☐ Sawubona (Zulu)
- ☐ Hallo (Norwegian)
- ☐ Zdravo (Bosnian)
- ☐ Ciao bello/bella (Italian)
- ☐ Hallå (Swedish)
- ☐ Alo (Haitian)
- ☐ Përshëndetje (Albanian)
- ☐ Aloha (Hawaiian)
- ☐ Privet (Russian)
- ☐ Kumusta (Tagalog)
- ☐ Shalom (Hebrew)
- ☐ Hi - are you there?
- ☐ Are you asleep yet?

- Hello sleepyhead - are you awake?
- Rise and Shine :)
- How's my favorite <brother/sister/mother/teacher> today?
- Don't be shy... just say hi ;)
- How you do, my sweet baboo?
- Where is <name>?

Let's Get Together Texts

These texting quips and scripts are easy ideas, ways, and suggestions that you can send to try and set a time/day to get together with the receiver.

Many of the texting scripts below are open-ended so that the receiver can choose what works with their schedule. Ex. What's your schedule like this week? Other sample scripts below give options for the receiver to choose from. Ex. Are you free Wednesday afternoon or Thursday evening?

The easiest way is to pick a topic from their opener response and segway from that. So if we continue with the sample text thread from the opener conversation, it may look like:

> Do you like Thai food? What's your favorite dish?

> Love Thai... especially coconut curry!

> Oooo I didn't learn that one! Do you know of any good spots? I'd love to try it - maybe we can figure out how they make theirs ;)

While conversations can flow in many directions, below is a 'Get Together' template for conversations:

'Let's Get Together' Template:

1. Select an Opener Text
2. Receiver's <response>
3. Select a 'Get Together' text
4. Receiver's <response>
5. Confirm their response with a reaction and select a Closer text.

GET TOGETHER FOR DRINKS/FOOD

Use the checkboxes to track which are your favourites or that you've used.

- ☐ Would you like to grab a bite to eat? I know a great hideaway place.

- ☐ Are you open for a coffee or drink this week? Would love to chat and get to know you better. :)

- ☐ Are you free for dinner sometime?

- ☐ I'm really craving <food i.e. sushi>. Know of any good spots? You want to come?

- ☐ Work has been nuts and I could totally blow off some steam. Are you up for a drink?

- ☐ Wednesday at 8pm... dinner. I'll pick you up ;)

- ☐ Let's do happy hour this week - what night are you free?

- ☐ I have a bottle of <beverage> with your name are on it.

- ☐ So I know it's super last minute, but I'll be in your area later today if you're up for a drink? No pressure!

- ☐ I've just heard of a new restaurant I'm dying to try... they supposedly have the best <food i.e. Italian>. You game?

- ☐ I hate that we keep missing each other - let me know when you're free for a coffee... maybe Thursday?

- ☐ I can't think of a good reason to go out to celebrate, but it's someone's birthday somewhere right now, and we don't want to be rude right? Let's grab a drink and toast to that ;)

GET TOGETHER FOR EVENT/ACTIVITY

Use the checkboxes to track which are your favourites or that you've used.

- ☐ Are you free on Saturday? I'm going <event i.e. a co-workers wedding reception> and can take a +1 - any interest? Don't make me brave it alone :)

- ☐ Hey! So I just scored extra tickets to <event i.e. the Bruno Mars concert>... I'm so excited!! Are you up for going?

- ☐ I know you need a break... so I've booked ___. Tell me you can get away?

- ☐ Have you seen the exhibit coming up at the museum? If you want to check it out sometime, let me know - I'd love to go!

- ☐ I'm dying to see <movie/theater/concert i.e. Avengers 13>... want to go?

- ☐ The weather looks fantastic this weekend! Let's take advantage of it and <activity i.e. have a picnic at the beach>!

- ☐ The weather doesn't look too promising this weekend... you up for a movie? Or bowling? I don't know... think of something indoors lol

- ☐ I've always wanted to go see some of the local sites... do you own a fanny pack? Let's buy 99 cent souvenirs and play tourists this weekend!

- ☐ Let's link up this weekend... the weather looks great for <activity i.e. a hike>!

☐ You're busy. I'm busy. Let's multi-task and do a study date? As long as you promise not to distract me... too much ;)

☐ There's a few of us heading out on <day i.e. Thursday>, you're welcome to join us if you'd like?

GET TOGETHER FOR CASUAL/GENERAL OCCASIONS

Use the checkboxes to track which are your favourites or that you've used.

☐ What are you up to this week... it'd be great to see you!

☐ Playful text and emoticons aside... let's pick a day to meet up :) How's your schedule this week?

☐ My fingers are tired from too much texting! lol... let's carry this conversation on in person—is after work good for you?

☐ My schedule is crazy but I'd still love to get together. Would Wed afternoon or Thur evening work? Let's make this happen :)

☐ Are you up for a little fun this week? ;)

☐ Let me know when you're free... I miss your face! :)

☐ Can you come out and play tonight?

☐ There's a few of us heading out - you're welcome to join if you'd like?

GET TOGETHER FOR A NIGHT IN

Use the checkboxes to track which are your favourites or that you've used.

- ☐ I'm loving this <chilly/rainy> weather... fancy a night in with some pizza and a Netflix marathon?

- ☐ As my way of saying thank you, I'd love to make a nice dinner for you and show off my cooking skills ;) What night works?

- ☐ Thursday night... 7pm. My place. Don't be late!

- ☐ Game night at mine? Call the troops!

- ☐ I have a new recipe I've been wanting to try... care to be my guinea pig? If it's terrible, we can always order in

- ☐ I really need some help with <item i.e. assembling a new IKEA chair, planning a budget, decorating>... I remember you said you're good at things like that right? Would you be able to help me?

- ☐ Movie ✔ Popcorn buttered ✔ Fuzzy blanket ✔ You? Come and join me ;)

- ☐ Just get your arse over here... now! ;)

Questions That Create Deeper Connections

Many times we want to build deeper connections with other people to build better friendships and relationships. These sample texting scripts can help do just that. The questions range in intimacy level starting with easier ones and ending with more personal questions.

Questions asked in an effort to get to know someone better, are typically better if they are open-ended because it gives the receiver an opportunity to express themselves. These quips and scripts are worded to do just that - to get the receiver thinking and start to open up more about their thoughts and feelings.

After a few exchanges, you may want to try a Call Me script or a Get Together script. It's easier to truly get to know someone by talking with them face-to-face or over the phone.

Note that in the conversation template the opener is listed as optional, based on the deeper question you ask. You may just want to brighten their day with a nice distraction and help get their mind off of the doldrums of mundane activities.

> Hey... how's your day going?

> Good... stuck in meetings.

> I know how much you love those ;) If you could be anywhere else in the world right now, where would you be?

Deeper connection questions give a mental break and allow the receiver to daydream for a moment, and also help each of you discover what your values in life are. From this sample text exchange and deeper connection question, we may learn any of the following:

- Does the receiver prefer the solitude in the mountains or laying on a sunny beach?

- How do they like to unwind and relax?
- Are they adventurous?

Another sample text exchange could go like:

> Hey... how's your day going?

> Good... stuck in meetings.

> I know how much you love those ;) What helps you unwind after a stressful day at work?

Use the conversation template below and select a deeper connection question, to help discover more about each other and create a deeper bond.

Deeper Connection Conversation:

1. Send an opener: "hi!" (optional)
2. Send a deeper question text.
3. <Responses>...

DEEPER QUESTIONS QUIPS & SCRIPTS

Use the checkboxes to track which are your favourites or that you've used.

☐ Rather than being at <place i.e. work>, if money were no object, where would you be?

☐ What's the worst job you've ever had?

☐ Any upcoming travel plans this <season i.e. summer>?

☐ So what brought you to <city/state i.e. California>?

☐ How do you and <mutual friend> know each other... any good stories?

☐ What's a day like in your world?

☐ What do you do when you're not working?

☐ How do you like to spend your time?

☐ What are you reading currently? Any recommendations?

☐ What's the first concert you attended?

☐ If you could go anywhere in the world, where would it be?

☐ What's your favourite TV show? I've just binged watched <show>... it's so good.

☐ What's your favourite 90's show?

☐ What's the best Halloween costume you've ever had?

☐ What's your dream job?

☐ What was your very first job?

- What's something you're excited about that's coming up this year?

- What is your most-used emoji?

- If you could have a useless superpower, what would you pick?

- If you could win any award, real or fake, what would it be for?

- Did you have any favourite subjects in school?

- What's your hidden talent?

- If you had to eat one thing at every meal for the rest of your life, what would you eat?

- Who would you cast in the starring role of your life movie?

- If you could spend an hour in someone else's shoes, who would it be?

- What's one thing your mother/father taught you that completely changed your life?

- What's been on your mind lately?

- What's the first career you dreamed of having as a kid?

- What's one of your favorite memories?

- Tell me something about you that might surprise other people?

- Who was your favorite teacher?

- What was your favorite subject in school? Why?

- What makes you feel extremely happy?

☐ What advice would you give your younger self?

☐ If you could snap your fingers and instantly be an expert at something, what would it be in?

☐ What does success mean to you?

☐ What's the best piece of advice you ever got?

☐ Where is your happy place?

☐ If you could invite 3 people, dead or alive, to a dinner party, who would they be, and why?

☐ How can someone win a gold star with you?

☐ What energizes you and gets you excited? What qualities do you value the most in the people?

☐ Would you ever want to be famous?

☐ What does your dream day look like?

☐ If you didn't have to sleep, what would you do with the extra time?

☐ What's your guilty pleasure?

☐ Has anything ever happened to you that you couldn't explain?

☐ What are you legitimately terrible at?

☐ Tell me 3 adjectives to describe yourself... go!

☐ What's on your bucket list in life?

☐ What did you have to give up to achieve your current level of success?

☐ What are you grateful for today?

☐ If there's anything you could 'do over' in life, what would it be?

☐ Is there anything that really scares you?

Texts to Flirt and Build Attraction

Texting can be a great way for flirty messages, letting each other know you're interested, and for fueling that fire when you can't be together. There's a whole method to keeping the attraction alive over texting, and these texts can help fan the flames for new flirty love interests or long-standing couples.

The key to these text messages, it that they can and should be personalized to the person you are sending them to. So take a moment and think about the receiver and why you love this person... what are the little details you've noticed about them?

The twinkle in their soulful eyes, the way they laugh, that feeling you get being near them. Tap into that energy before selecting a text message script.

'Flirty' Template:

1. Send an opener: "hi!"
2. <Response> "Hello".
3. Send a Flirty text.

FLIRTY QUIPS & SCRIPTS

Use the checkboxes to track which are your favourites or that you've used.

- ☐ You have the nicest <feature i.e. eyes>.
- ☐ I can't stop thinking about <little thing they do i.e your laugh>
- ☐ You make me smile 😊
- ☐ You're the most amazing man I've ever met
- ☐ I feel like the luckiest girl on the planet when I'm with you.
- ☐ I love how it feels just being with you...
- ☐ You make my heart smile <3
- ☐ It's amazing how good it feels knowing that you're mine
- ☐ You give me the warm fuzzies xo
- ☐ I still get butterflies when I think of you. x
- ☐ I see you and it's like the temperature rises 100 degrees! I don't know what you do to me ;)
- ☐ I'm so glad that I'm yours, and you're mine.
- ☐ You inspire me to be a better person. x
- ☐ I love it when ....
- ☐ You looked so amazing last night xo
- ☐ I dreamt of you last night ;)

☐ I'm so proud to be on your arm.

☐ I'm so proud to have you on my arm.

☐ Your smile lights up the whole room :)

☐ You're my rock, thank you babe, because I really need that right now.

☐ Just thinking of you xo

☐ Just wanted to say hi :) Please continue with your regularly scheduled day xo

☐ Sending you warm thoughts xo

☐ You rock my world like Def Leppard did in 1987.

☐ You're such a charmer 😉

☐ So... would you rather be working right now or with me?

☐ I'm in a dilemma... I can't stop thinking about you. What should I do?

☐ You look amazing in that new shirt 🔥

☐ Green is definitely you color 😋

☐ I'm bored... are you up for an adventure??

☐ Good luck on your <game/show> tonight! You'll do awesome and look sexy doing it 😉

☐ We just arrived in <place i.e. Cancun>! Ugh I wish you were here! It'd be so much more fun 😋

☐ Happy Birthday! If you could have one wish, what would it be? 😉

☐ Come over, I have all your favorites… pizza, beer, and of course, ME!

☐ OMG, you were amazing last night 😘

☐ I can't wait to see you later… I think you'll like what you see 😉

☐ Hmm, should I wear the red panties or the black ones? Any thoughts?

☐ I've been thinking about you all day… it hasn't all been rated G either 😘

☐ Send me a picture 😉

☐ Sweet dreams….with me in them 😉

☐ I'm just laying in bed, bored. Care to join?

☐ Let's hang out tonight. I promise you won't regret it 😉

☐ I just woke up and you're already on my mind. 💗

☐ I love a man/woman that can (fill in the blank).

☐ I know you're busy this week, but can you add me on to your to-do list?

☐ I want to take you home and pleasure you in ways you didn't know were possible.

☐ You make me feel so (fill in the blank).

☐ I love your lips… I can't wait to taste them again.

☐ Come over. Now.

☐ Dang, you look extra hot today 🔥🔥🔥

- Have you been working out?

- Mmm, come over here. I want to touch you.

- I can't wait to see you XOXO

- Guess what I'm wearing right now

- I was telling my friends about you... they're so jealous 😊

- I had a dream about you last night

- I've been a bad girl today... I might need a spanking 😊

- Talk dirty to me.

- Don't waste all of your energy today, you'll need some for later ;)

- Ugh, I was rushing out of the house and totally forgot to wear a bra today!

- I found my old cheerleading outfit. It still fits...

- I've had a horrible day and need to unwind... care to help? 😊

- Can you guess the color of the underwear I'm wearing?

- I've never met anyone that can (fill in the blank) as well as you.

- If I were with you right now, what would we be doing?

- I'm trying to fall asleep but my brain can't stop thinking about you!

How to Suggest a Phone Call

Like Blondie sang in the 1980 hit, "Call Me!", these texts offer ways to suggest, encourage, and ask to have a phone conversation.

Sometimes you want the other person to call… whether it's a love interest, co-worker, friend or family member. Perhaps you've tried reaching out to them and they haven't responded, you've been playing endless phone tag, or really just need to talk to someone.

Below are three sample 'Call Me' text messages which all show that you're looking to build a deeper connection and relationship. Sometimes there is no end goal and you really just want to connect and say hi, you're tired of endlessly texting, or want to hear the person's voice. There are plenty of Quips & Scripts to give you ideas.

> Hey… I've had a rough day and would love to just chat. You around?

> I miss the sound of your voice. :-)

> Just got amazing news! Call me when you have a minute!

Use the 'Call Me' conversation template below as a basis to move from a texting conversation to a phone conversation. You may opt out of revealing your goal or intention, because you may want to wait and discuss it with them directly to gauge their reaction.

However, if you want to give them a heads up on the topic needed to be discussed and give them time to think about it, then include step 3 and let them know what you'd like to discuss over the phone.

'Call Me' Conversation Template:

1. Send an "Opener" text.
2. <Response> "Hello".
3. Select a "Call Me" text.
4. <Response>
5. Select a "Closer" text.

CALL ME QUIPS & SCRIPTS

Use the checkboxes to track which are your favourites or that you've used.

☐ I'd really like to hear your thoughts on <topic>.

☐ Are you available later today to talk about <topic>?

☐ I'm headed out soon but wanted to discuss <topic> with you today. Do you have time now?

- ☐ I know you're busy but let me know when you're free to talk?

- ☐ I miss your voice... can you chat? xo

- ☐ So I'd love to move this conversation over to the phone... what do you think?

- ☐ I just got the most amazing news! Call me when you have a second!

- ☐ It's important to me that we talk about this, because I don't want any miscommunications.

- ☐ Can you call and wish me goodnight? ;)

- ☐ I'd love to hear your voice as the last thing before I drift off to sleep ;) call me!

- ☐ My fingers are tired of texting... are you free to chat?

- ☐ Let's chat about this - call me in 5.

- ☐ Can you talk?

- ☐ This is too long to type - can you chat?

- ☐ Give me a call when you can - I'd love to catch up and hear what's been going on with you!

- ☐ Are you around this afternoon to talk?

How to Say NO

There are times when you're not interested in someone, not interesting in an activity, need to say no, have too much going on, etc. but it can still be hard for some people to say no. These Quips & Scripts are geared towards letting the receiver **know** that you mean **no**.

'Saying No' Conversation Template:

1. Received an opener with a request or asking a question..
2. Select a 'Saying No' text message.

3. Send a closer if desired.

SAYING NO QUIPS & SCRIPTS

Use the checkboxes to track which are your favourites or that you've used.

☐ Sorry I already have plans! No thanks.

☐ It was nice meeting you! I'm sorry but I didn't feel that 'spark' or chemistry I'm looking for though. Best of luck in your search

☐ That sounds fun but I can't. Have a great time!

☐ I'm totally booked that day and can't help. Sorry!

☐ No thanks, I'm just not interested but am flattered that you invited me.

☐ Sorry not for me!

☐ No thank you.

☐ Thanks for thinking of me but I'm not available.

☐ I am swamped and can't get away.

☐ Wish I could go! Have fun without me!

- ☐ Sorry, super busy. I'll reach out when I have a minute.
- ☐ I'm tied up all day and can't :-(
- ☐ NnnnOOoooo!!!
- ☐ Mmmmm let me think about it…. Nope!! Can't.
- ☐ Nope. Nada. Zilch. Can't.
- ☐ Thanks but no.

When You are Concerned for their Well-being

There are times when you're really concerned for someone's well-being or safety. Perhaps they've crossed your mind because you know they're in a difficult situation and you want to offer your support.

These Quips & Scripts are geared towards getting the receiver to open up about their feelings and emotions, and what's going on in their life.

'Concerned' Conversation Template:

1. Send an opener: "hi!"
2. <Response>
3. Select a 'Concerned' text message.

CONCERNED QUIPS & SCRIPTS

Use the checkboxes to track which are your favourites or that you've used.

☐ You've been on my heart lately... is everything okay?

☐ I was thinking of you today, how is everything going?

☐ How are you? You seemed upset <yesterday>... is anything on your mind?

☐ Praying for you my friend ((hugs)).

☐ So tell me though... really, how are you? I'm concerned about you.

☐ I hope you know you can always talk to me... ok?

☐ I'm here for you if you ever want to talk.

☐ How are you feeling about <situation>? I've been thinking of you.

☐ I know this is a tough time - my mom used to say tough times don't last but tough people do, and you're one tough cookie!

☐ Are there any updates on <situation>? Let me know if you need any help.

☐ You are so incredibly loved by so many... I hope you know we're all here to help you through this.

☐ I know you'll make it through this and maybe someday we can all look back at this and laugh?

☐ I'm pulling for you! You're gonna make it!!!

☐ I know you're going through a rough patch. Let me know if there's anything I can do to help cheer you up :) ((hugs)) my friend.

☐ How are you feeling today, any better?

Responding to Confusing or Offending Texts

Suppose you received a text message that you're just not sure how to interpret, what they really meant, or perhaps you're even slightly offended.

These Quips & Scripts can be used to help clarify the intended meaning behind a text message and understand what was trying to be said.

In these cases, because there is already a misunderstanding underway, it's often helpful and necessary to discuss the situation over the phone or in-person to avoid further miscommunications and the texting pitfalls discussed in earlier chapters.

Send back one of the sample messages below, followed up with a 'Call Me' text to help clear the air in a positive way.

CONFUSED/OFFENDED QUIPS & SCRIPTS

Use the checkboxes to track which are your favourites or that you've used.

☐ Huh???

☐ I'm not sure I understand what you mean?

☐ Feeling conflustered by that... lol 😊 What???

- That last text confused me...

- Maybe I need more caffeine – what are you trying to say?

- I'm not sure I know what you mean by that... can we chat?

- Can you explain that differently? I don't get it.

- What? I'm not getting it.

- I'm not sure I'm understanding you. Can you call me?

- Was that an auto-corrected message? It doesn't make sense to me?

- I don't think I'm understanding you... are you available to talk?

- I've been feeling 'off' after your message... do you have time to chat so I can get this off my chest?

- I'd really like to clear the air on this.

- Can you explain that more?

- What do you mean? I don't understand.

How to say You're Sorry or Express Sympathies

No one is perfect. We've all messed up and have had to send messages to smooth things over. These messages can also be used if the receiver has suffered loss in their family, tragic illness, or just when you want to express condolences and sympathies.

Many times the receiver of the message may need time to process the event or circumstances. So there tends to be a higher chance of no response in this case. If there is a response it could be in anger "Why did you do this??!!" or "Why did this have to happen??!", it could be in sadness, or it could be in forgiveness.

Whatever the response is, remember that the receiver may be feeling hurt and vulnerable. Be sensitive to their needs and respond accordingly.

APOLOGY QUIPS & SCRIPTS

Use the checkboxes to track which are your favourites or that you've used.

- ☐ I'm so sorry ☹

- ☐ I wanted to let you know that I really heard what you said and respect it. I don't want to disappoint you again... being human I probably will, but it won't be from ___. I'm sorry.

- ☐ I'm so sorry I've let you down and I want to make this right.

- ☐ How can I make this up to you?

- ☐ This is important to me to get it right and I hope you know I'm sorry. Can we please talk?

- ☐ I'm sorry I've disappointed you. I don't want to do it again...ever.

- ☐ Please let me know how I can make this up to you.

☐ Even heaven knows that I have offended you but I'm just realizing it now. Please forgive me and let's reconcile for a new beginning.

☐ I'm not proud of my character or of what I did, but I have learned my lessons and am deeply sorry.

☐ I was thinking that I was doing the right thing not knowing that I was hurting someone so close to me. Please forgive my ignorance and let me try to make things right.

☐ Life was so beautiful and perfect with you and I'd love to get back to that place. Are you open to working towards that?

☐ I'm sorry I hurt you.

☐ I'm sorry I've disappointed you. I've let myself down too, but really want to learn and grow from this.

☐ I can't express how sorry I am right now please find a place in your heart to forgive me.

☐ We've gone through situations worse than this, please don't let this spoil our happiness and love.

☐ I know I have offended you but right now all I want is an opportunity to show you the positive side of me, I'm sorry.

☐ I will not challenge your decision because what I did was wrong, but I am asking you for an opportunity to fix all the damages that I have caused you.

☐ I didn't realize how rude and lousy I was until now. I am hopeful you can give this another chance.

☐ What I did is unthinkable but please forgive me. Let's reconcile and work at getting back to being us?

☐ Forgive me please?

☐ I never realized the impact that one mistake could have on a relationship we have built for so long, please forgive me. I have committed a great sin.

☐ I am sure your feelings towards me have changed because of what I did but am using this opportunity to asking you to forgive me. I have identified my mistakes and promise to never ever do it again.

☐ I feel like the worst person in the whole world. I'm so sorry and promise I'll never do it again. Forgive me babe.

☐ Where should I send the "I'm sorry, please forgive me. I love you endlessly" flowers?

☐ I am extremely sorry for hurting you and ask for your forgiveness.

☐ I am sorry for arguing with you, you know that I only want the best for both of us. Please forgive me baby.

☐ I am sorry if I'm being a bit clingy. It is just that I can't stop thinking about you.

☐ I am very sorry. I did a grave thing in hurting you yesterday.

- ☐ I don't know what to say or do, but I hope you can look past this and forgive me.

- ☐ I hope you accept my apology, for it comes not only with the deepest regrets but with intentions so pure, that it'd make Jesus proud.

- ☐ I may have been wrong but if I don't have "us", I'll never be right.

- ☐ I promise I'll think before I speak next time. I need you in my life and I'm very sorry.

- ☐ If I could, I would take back all the things I did to hurt you. I am sorry.

- ☐ If you leave me alone, I'd self-destruct. Please accept my apology.

- ☐ I'm heartbroken and feel very bad for what I did. I know I will never be able to make it up to you, but let me begin with an apology. Tell me what to do after that?

- ☐ I am sorry sweetheart, I will never lie to you. Ever.

- ☐ Our relationship is so important to me. Please forgive my stupidity and forget what I said/did.

- ☐ I hope that saying I'm sorry will revive our relationship. I miss you and I love you.

- ☐ Take your time. I'll wait forever, if that's how long it'll take for you to forgive me. I love you.

☐ You are the light in my life; without you my world is dark. Please forgive me.

☐ Forgive this fool who can't live without you.

☐ You mean the world to me and I will do everything I can to make this up to you. I'm sorry and I hope you will forgive me, won't you?

SYMPATHY QUIPS & SCRIPTS

Use the checkboxes to track which are your favourites or that you've used.

☐ My deepest sympathies to you and yours

☐ I'm so sorry to hear the news… please call me if you need anything.

☐ My heart goes out to you right now.

☐ Prayers and ((hugs)) my dear friend

☐ Sending much love and prayers for you and the family

☐ I can't imagine what you're going through, but please know I'm here if you need me.

☐ Our thoughts are with you right now.

☐ :'(I'm so sorry

☐ Is there anything I can do to help?

☐ Sending you all of my love… I wish there was more I could do. If there is, please let me know.

- Even if you need an escape - a drink, movie, dinner, whatever... just let me know.

- His/her life touched so many people with kindness and left a beautiful legacy.

- I'll always remember his/her laugh and the way they made other people smile.

- He/She had such a full life surrounded by people they love... that's a true blessing.

Dealing with Bad Behaviors

In every relationship, there are behaviors that come up that we want to address. Behavioral studies have shown that positive reinforcements can be beneficial to encouraging things that we like in relationships, while discouraging things that disturb us.

Based on using positivity, there are two techniques which can be helpful in addressing negative behaviors: The Praise Technique and The Positivity Sandwich.

THE PRAISE TECHNIQUE

This technique coincides with Improving the Text within your Texts chapter and puts the power of our words into practice, using positive and encouraging messages to build someone up.

Putting the Praise Technique into practice requires focusing on the positive aspects of each other and our daily lives, and comes into play during those moments we recognize something good, a positive trait, a compliment, or behavior we want to encourage.

In those moments, share that compliment in an authentic way. That compliment is internalized by the receiver and that good behavior is reinforced.

A few examples of the Praise Technique are below:

> It was so great to hear your voice tonight... I love when you call me. x

> Thank you for helping me yesterday. It means so much to me to know that you've got my back.

> I love it when you take extra time with the kids - they do too. I can see it in their smiles :-)

Take time each day to recognize the good and positive things in your world and simply acknowledge them. When you share a praise, you are putting positive vibrant energy into the world and creating a ripple effect that can extend further than you'd imagine. In addition, that positive energy is also internalized and may boost your mood and energy level.

THE POSITIVITY SANDWICH

The "Positivity Sandwich" can address a specific behavior that we find undesirable. It still requires thinking of two positive traits that we want to reinforce. These can be anything related to the person themselves, the event, or the venue, etc. Then we insert the negative behavior in the middle.

In dealing with negative behaviors, it's important to review 'Improving the Text within your Texts' chapter, and be mindful of the 3-step approach mentioned in that chapter before drafting the positivity sandwich.

Texting pitfalls to be especially aware of with bad behavior texts are the avoid texting when angry and the multiple topic pitfalls. Avoid being overly emotional here and pick the main behavior you want to address, not a laundry lists of faults.

A few examples of Positivity Sandwiches are listed below:

I know you are such a hard worker and I really respect that about you, but if you can let me know when you're running late, I can plan my day better. That'd be such a huge help to me!

> Babe you have the sexiest voice ♡ So when you say you're going to call and don't, it upsets me because not only do I want to hear your voice but it's also important to me to be able to trust what you say. Plus we always have the best conversations… I just love talking to you. x

> You're work reports are also so detailed and thorough. If you can proof them a little better for any typos though that'd help me out a great deal. Overall though you're doing a great job!!

Closing a Conversation

These sample Quips & Scripts will properly end a conversation, and signal to the other person or people that you won't be available right away if they immediately text back.

In some cases, closers are optional, but when in doubt it's better to err on the side of caution and send a closing text, so the receiver isn't left wondering what happened to you.

CLOSING QUIPS & SCRIPTS

Use the checkboxes to track which are your favourites or that you've used.

- ☐ Later!
- ☐ TTYL (Talk to you later) *not for use in professional/client setting
- ☐ BRB (Be right back) * not for use in professional/client setting
- ☐ Ciao bello/bella! (Italian)
- ☐ Okay gotta run... talk to you soon. x
- ☐ I'm headed out now. Let's chat later?
- ☐ Talk to you soon!
- ☐ Byyyyye :)
- ☐ Thank you, we'll be in touch
- ☐ Have a great afternoon!
- ☐ Let's catch up again soon :)
- ☐ Okay thanks - I'll get back to you soon.
- ☐ I'll call you with any questions. Thanks!
- ☐ Alright I have to run - see you later!
- ☐ G'night x

- ☐ Adios mi Amigo/Amiga
- ☐ Sleep well!
- ☐ Aloha!
- ☐ Pleasant dreams - Don't let the bed bugs bite!
- ☐ Have a good day! Chat soon :)
- ☐ See you tomorrow :)
- ☐ Heading out - make sure and have fun tonight!
- ☐ Chat to you soon!
- ☐ TTYS (Talk to you soon) *not for use in professional/client setting
- ☐ I've got to get back to <activity i.e. work>. Have a good one :)
- ☐ Ok, I hope we can chat soon. x
- ☐ Will you be around in <time i.e. 2 hours>? I'm tied up until around then.
- ☐ Thanks for talking with me!
- ☐ Ok - I'll get in touch with you soon.
- ☐ See ya soon sweetheart
- ☐ Later gator!
- ☐ Have a good evening :)
- ☐ Adieu (French)
- ☐ Parting is such sweet sorrow :'(
- ☐ I hope to talk to you again soon. x
- ☐ Farewell :)

- ☐ Until we see each other again x

- ☐ So long for now!

- ☐ Bon voyage :)

- ☐ See you!

- ☐ Take care!

- ☐ Catch you later

- ☐ Goodnight!

- ☐ Later Gator

- ☐ Peace. Out.

- ☐ Sayonara, sucker! :-p

- ☐ auf Wiedersehen (German)

- ☐ Shalom <3 (Hebrew)

ABOUT THE AUTHOR

Through both education and professional experience, Elizabeth Rossi has studied all forms of writing including technical documentation, television pilots and scripts, feature film screenplays, marketing blogs and product copy, press releases, creative writing and non-fiction.

She is a cum laude graduate of the University of Pittsburgh and has since written over 80 guide books and manuals, five feature length screenplays, three television pilots, and countless online articles covering a range of themes.

The mediums and topics of writing which continue to expand, give a breadth and depth to her communication, and she is happy to teach and share this knowledge with others to help people improve their own communication skills, and express their ideas, feelings, and emotions in the best way possible.

Please visit Elizabeth's website for the latest news, information, and additional upcoming projects:
www.errossi.com

Made in United States
Orlando, FL
18 September 2023

37046663R00091